SOCIAL STRATEGY
AND
CORPORATE
STRUCTURE

NEIL W. CHAMBERLAIN

Studies of the Modern Corporation
Graduate School of Business
Columbia University

MACMILLAN PUBLISHING CO., INC.
NEW YORK

Collier Macmillan Publishers
LONDON

Macmillan Publishing Co., Inc.
866 Third Avenue, New York, N.Y. 10022

Collier Macmillan Canada, Ltd.

Library of Congress Catalog Card Number: 81-67989

Printed in the United States of America

printing number

1 2 3 4 5 6 7 8 9 10

Library of Congress Cataloging in Publication Data

Chamberlain, Neil W.
    Social strategy and corporate structure.

    (Studies of the modern corporation)
    Includes index.
      1. Industry—Social aspects—United States.
2. Corporations—Social aspects—United States.
3. Industrial organization—United States. 4. Industrial management—United States.   I. Title.   II. Series.
HD60.5.U5C476   658.4'08   81-67989
ISBN 13: 978-1-4165-7645-7   AACR2
ISBN 10: 1-4165-7645-2

SOCIAL STRATEGY AND CORPORATE STRUCTURE

STUDIES OF THE MODERN CORPORATION
Graduate School of Business, Columbia University

The Program for Studies of the Modern Corporation is devoted to the advancement and dissemination of knowledge about the corporation. Its publications are designed to stimulate inquiry, research, criticism, and reflection. They fall into three categories: works by outstanding businessmen, scholars, and professional men from a variety of backgrounds and academic disciplines; annotated and edited selections of business literature; and business classics that merit republication. The studies are supported by outside grants from private business, professional, and philanthropic institutions interested in the program's objectives.

RICHARD EELLS
Director

Contents

Contents

Preface

THERE is a great deal of discussion these days about restructuring the corporation. Many people—both inside and outside business—believe that the corporation requires organizational change if it is to function effectively within a changed social environment. It is a matter not only of a revised socially acceptable behavior (strategy) but also of a revised and appropriate corporate structure.

This study builds on that view. In some respects it is the American companion volume to my *Forces of Change in Western Europe* (1980), which dealt with some of the same issues in the very different institutional setting of western Europe.

I am grateful for the financial support of the Faculty Research Fund of the Graduate School of Business, Columbia University, in pursuing this interest.

NEIL W. CHAMBERLAIN
Armand G. Erpf Professor
of the Modern Corporation

New York City
April 1981

SOCIAL STRATEGY AND CORPORATE STRUCTURE

1

The Uncertain Relation between Business and Society

The corporation in America was first and foremost a political expression performing a public economic function. The colonies transplanted a mercantilist European society. The central tenet of mercantilism was the integration of the social order within the nation-state, which had become the parochial and secular substitute for the declining Roman Catholic church. The advancement of the state was intended to contribute to the welfare of its people, and that political objective affected the character of the state's instrumentalities. Thus, in colonial America, no less than in the metropolitan countries of Europe, the state created corporations for public purposes. The purely private business affairs of the colonists, more restricted in scale and scope, were carried on chiefly by individuals or by unincorporated joint-stock companies of a local nature.

The Corporation in the Early United States

Neither independence nor Adam Smith's great antimercantilist polemic *The Wealth of Nations*, which emerged in the same year, wrought any radical change in public attitudes toward the corpora-

1

tion as a political instrument. Mercantilist views on the need for government to promote the social welfare hung on in the newly created United States for fifty years or more. No longer, however, were there the preclusive powers of an overseas imperial government, nor did the new federal government exercise much of an inhibitive role. Under the constitutional principle of states' rights, state governments moved into the business of chartering their own corporations. Each corporation required a special act of the state legislature, tailored to the specific purpose being promoted.

By the turn of the nineteenth century more than three hundred business corporations had been created. Two-thirds were concerned with inland navigation, turnpikes, and toll bridges. The remainder included insurance companies, commercial banks, and public services (e.g., administering the water supply and docks). As the historian Stuart Bruchey observed: "These business corporations were no more exclusively profit-seeking associations than the chartered joint-stock companies with which the English had pioneered in the settlement of America. They were, in fact, quasi-public agencies of the state." He quoted a Massachusetts charter of 1818 that created "a corporation *and body politic*" for the purpose of milling flour.[1] The special privileges accorded such corporations were premised on the social services they rendered: the dedication of private capital and entrepreneurial effort to the public interest. Other investigators have underlined this political character of the early corporation. John P. Davis, in his classic two-volume history of the corporation, noted that "it was not considered justifiable to create corporations for any purpose not clearly public in nature; each application was considered by itself, and if favorably, was followed by a legislative act of incorporation."[2] Oscar Handlin commented that "at its origin in Massachusetts, the corporation was conceived as an agency of the government, endowed with public attributes, exclusive privileges, and political power, and designed to serve a social function for the State."[3]

After 1815 an increase in economic opportunity projected the country into what, in contemporary terminology, would be called the takeoff into sustained economic growth. The moving West became more closely integrated with the industrially expanding East. A surge in immigration, especially of the Irish and Germans, increased the pool of both consumers and workers. A concomitant, yeasty egalitarianism led to movements in the several states for abolition of property holder or taxpayer status to qualify for the vote;

2

admission of new states, formed out of the western territories and populated with rugged individualists, expanded an assertive electorate.

This spread of economic opportunity gave rise to a new class of economic adventurers in single-minded pursuit of wealth. The cult of the self-made man became the national symbol. In those heady days the self-created businessman was the very embodiment of democracy, contrasting with the members of the older eastern aristocratic families who had inherited their privileges. The changed climate was not without effect on the political concept of the corporation.

First, the practice of issuing corporate charters by special legislative act came to be viewed with suspicion and distaste. For one thing, it smacked of privilege: individuals with well-placed contacts, favorable social standing, and economic advantage clearly had an inside track on a state's grant of corporate rights. Even though that grant was premised on the rendering of a public service it nevertheless entailed private profit and benefit. Egalitarian sentiment supported a legislature representing all equally.

A second shift in social attitude toward the corporation was perhaps even more important. In the spirit of the times economic development, a national objective, was a goal that could be promoted by Everyman. Adam Smith was coming into his own, winning recognition that the butcher, the baker, the candlestick maker—all seeking their private gain—were contributing to the national wealth and thus serving a public purpose. In serving a public purpose, they, too, merited the advantages of incorporation. In Davis's words, "Not only was it difficult to distinguish between public and private, but the view that individuals should have the freest possible opportunities to create wealth encouraged the presumption that every business was of public importance in the respect that it might increase the aggregate wealth of society."[4] Private enterprise had become public purpose.

The consequence for the corporation of this changing social context was remarkable. Although there had been some early flirtation with general incorporation laws, obviating the necessity of special legislative acts, movement in this direction now swelled. At least half a dozen states had passed general incorporation laws prior to the Civil War. And the notion that public purpose was served by private profit seeking gave ample rationale to this more open access to the corporate form, with its attendant advantages.

Private profit seeking has characterized societies in almost every age, as R. H. Tawney pointed out, but what was new about the nineteenth-century development, and especially its American expression, was the unabashed identification of private with public good and the widespread embrace of material advancement as embodying the highest democratic good. This value orientation shaped both American society and the American landscape. Law and business practice emphasized the privacy of person and property and gave to the corporation the constitutional rights of those persons who had formed it. After all, the federal constitution had made no special provision for such an institution. Business relations —the relations between the institutionalized person of the corporation and the real persons with whom it dealt—rested on voluntary contract, volition assumed to be equal on both sides. Such voluntary relations were largely unsupervised by the state as to their effects on the contracting parties or on third parties—even whole communities. Cities and nature, people and resources, became appropriate arenas for the economic exploits of private adventurers, whether single entrepreneurs or incorporated associates.

Expanding Corporations and Their Impact

The consequence of this transformation of the corporation from public service provider to private profit seeker became more evident after the Civil War with the development of a national market based on an expanding transportation network. The more enterprising corporations grew in size, enlarged their financial base, and changed their organizational form and managerial functions. In effect the corporation, which sought to seize the economic opportunities offered by the amalgamation of pockets of population into a vast and virtual empire, had to pull up its local roots, separating itself from a community in which its managers were familiar civic figures, subject to the constraints of neighbors' opinions, and loosening ties with the state that issued the corporate charter. Abandoning this limited field of operations, the national corporation could obtain its charter in any state as a license to do business anywhere in the nation. Autonomous in its actions under the permissive philosophy of private initiative, the national corporation, with its subsidiaries and satellites, was free to move in and out of communities as suited its operations. With its behavior justified by the political

4

principle that whatever contributed to economic development achieved public purposes, the national corporation could view social communities and the physical environment as malleable materials to be shaped to its own pecuniary advantage.

The enormity of this continental challenge spawned a race of titans capable of measuring up to the new standard. Cities like Detroit, Gary, Chicago, St. Louis, Omaha, and Denver could be thrown up almost like stage sets, outfitted to satisfy corporate balance sheets. Technology—building from Eli Whitney's insightful use of interchangeable parts in the early nineteenth century—was pushed at an accelerating pace; one discovery paved the way for another. In an early version of Mao's hundred blooming flowers, backyard laboratories sprang up wherever there were backyards. Soon the basement inventor was replicated on a vast scale within the nationalizing corporations: Steinmetz and General Electric became the paradigm.

New industries emerged—automobile, rubber and tire, electrical, pharmaceutical. The race of titans gave way to more impersonal and institutionalized divisions of the large corporations, each with a mission and a budget—to invent, to develop commercially, to produce efficiently and profitably, to create appetites for the more and the different. Raw and processed materials followed the same pattern—steel mills that quickly dwarfed those of England, from which they had taken their inspiration; oil derricks hastily assembled to bring the new fuel to use abundantly and quickly, if also wastefully; massive machinery, eventually towering like Gothic cathedrals in the wilderness, for the purpose of extracting coal and minerals and in the process creating mountains of slag that would be left ominously behind. Like the materials-producing industries, the new manufacturing plants generated wastes on a scale proportionate to their output. Wastes could be discharged into rivers and lakes, deposited in landfills, or buried. In some instances the violation of social amenities was blatant enough to evoke—not always effectively—resentment and resistance: automobile graveyards stacked with the rusted bodies of junked cars; nauseous odors in the vicinity of plants using certain chemicals; and water so contaminated that the chlorination to make it safe for drinking made it unpalatable. In other cases toxic wastes buried in the ground or left in dump sites found their way, after the passage of years, into underground streams, where they endangered the health of nearby residents. The potential hazard may never have been suspected: the dump was available and there were few restrictions on the private use of land (there still are not in many states).

Thus, large-scale corporate industry affected society in two ways: the direct impact of the production process on the social and natural environment—the use of people and nature as resources for the benefit of the autonomous corporation, whose private gain was identified with public good; and the health hazards, pollution, and environmental despoliation for which no corporate responsibility—until recently—was assessed since these activities breeched no right of contract or fair usage of property and were incidental to the production process, which was itself wanted (corporate profits, workers' jobs, and community taxes all being at stake).

Moreover, the adverse effects of technological processes are often disputable: "Is the routine use of antibiotics in animal feed breeding medicine-resistant bacteria that will eventually cause untreatable diseases in humans?" *Business Week* asks. "No one seems to know for sure. . . . The stakes are huge. Although the $170 million annual market for animal-use antibiotics represents insignificant fractions of the total sale of such drug giants as American Cyanamid, Pfizer, and Diamond Shamrock, it forms the backbone of their agricultural sales divisions. . . . The nagging question, however, is whether continuing the use of feed antibiotics will yield cheap meat at the expense of good health."[5] An elderly woman living near a former industrial dumpsite that harbors residual asbestos, benzine, and other toxic substances, says perplexedly: "Chemicals are everywhere. One test will show that it's dangerous, one test will show that it's not. In this day and age, who do you believe?"[6]

The knotty problem of weighing economic advantage against social disadvantage, particularly in the face of scientific uncertainty, is perhaps most clearly illustrated by the case of nuclear power. But recent years have witnessed an increasing number of like industrial dilemmas: the effect of certain spray propellants on the ozone layer; the hothouse effect of carbon dioxide from increased coal burning to conserve scarce and expensive oil; the widespread use of herbicides containing dioxin, which has been called the most powerful carcinogen known; and a Pandora's box of suggested horrors capable of being visited on humankind by genetic engineering for industrial purposes. The unknowns involved are vigorously debated by scientists.

In the face of such scientific riddles, courts have at times taken the position that "the lives and health of people . . . in the circumstances of modern industrialism, are largely beyond self-protection."[7] But if this is so, who has responsibility for the public? Is responsibility rested in the corporation, whose value system stresses autonomous decisions directed to the business's own advantage? Is responsibility rested in the hands of government agents, who would have to create a vast network to oversee all corporate activity, granting or refusing their imprimatur often on the basis of inadequate or conflicting information? Is industrialization on a large scale a force so elemental, almost like nature itself, that it cannot be controlled in any meaningful sense?

Leo Marx surveyed the attitudes of American writers of the nineteen and twentieth centuries with respect to the impact of industrialism on society and constructed a vivid historic allegory entitled *The Machine in the Garden.*[8] From its discovery America embodied the myth of the garden—an Eden existing in reality. The myth had two versions: one, a primitivistic view—nature untouched, unspoiled, and provident; the other, a cultural view—nature left to itself tending as much to wilderness as to garden and requiring human care to realize the pastoral vision.

Into this idyllic conception of the New World intruded, in time, the machine, the steam engine, and above all, the railroad. The Industrial Revolution had started in England, it was true, but there the machine intruded into a formed, socialized setting, with classes, customs, and commerce already in place. In America, it intruded into the unspoiled Garden, the myth-dream of a recovered Eden.

For a while, the opposition between the two cultures—the pastoral and the technological—went unrecognized. The machine could be regarded as a product of the Enlightenment, enjoyed and praised for its capacity to supply harnessed power, allowing the husbandman to practice even more successfully his rural pursuit—divorced in thought from an urban, factory culture. Even when the recognition came that a machine society introduced competing values and social relations, there developed the philosophic-poetic-artistic vision of "the middle landscape." The machine could be harnessed to tasks that would improve the pastoral society—but it must be restrained at the point where, if allowed to expand further, it would itself dominate society.

Following this conception, the frontier West epitomized the barbaric wilderness of nature untamed. Europe was the overcivilized, overcommercialized, overurbanized, and overmechanized domain where the new technology had been allowed to rule. In between—

7

geographically, psychologically, and socially—lay settled America, still in a controllable stage of development: the middle landscape avoided the undesirable extremes.

The vision was static, and as technology expanded its hold under the driving force of unrestrained individualistic competition, American writers sought to confront the vision and the reality, the machine in the garden, in a way that reconciled pastoral sensibilities with modern technological advances. But reconciliation was impossible. American literature became distinguished by the dialectic, the discomfort, the disillusion of a deeply felt need to hold fast to natural goodness in the face of irresistible institutional forces. As Marx concluded his illuminating study: "To change the situation we require new symbols of possibility, and although the creation of those symbols is in some measure the responsibility of artists, it is in greater measure the responsibility of society. The machine's sudden entrance into the garden presents a problem that ultimately belongs not to art but to politics."[9]

Social Challenges to Corporate Autonomy

If corporate industrialism has had adverse as well as benign effects on society, requiring a reappraisal of their relationship, it is no less true that society has been undergoing transformations that have influenced the business corporation. These have largely to do with the pressures of population on resources and space. Relative scarcity has always been an issue, to be sure, but in most countries before industrialization the problem was contained by early indoctrination in an appropriate allocation of scarce goods by social class and function; since the spread of industrialization this problem has been finessed by the promise of economic growth in which all could share, even if not equally. Only within the past few decades—indeed, chiefly within the last decade—has the notion of absolute scarcity been debated. If we can safely say that few now subscribe to the concept of a definite limit on economic growth, we would have to add that many—including many reputable scientists—affirm that economic growth does have limits, even though not easily specified, and that continued indiscriminate growth may waste irreplaceable resources and permanently despoil the environment. It is the one measure of the seriousness with which we now view resource limits that air and water—once classic examples of free goods—have come to be appreciated as having their price, sometimes a high one.[10]

The soaring costs of energy in all forms have engendered the fear of a declining standard of consumption. Pressures to sustain economic growth—to maintain jobs and income, if not to add to affluence—have resulted in the use of lower quality, less accessible, higher cost raw materials (the Ricardian effect), raising prices and frustrations. The optimistic belief that new technologies will provide substitute products and processes is at best an article of faith and at worst ignores potentially damaging consequences of the substitutes (the industrialization effect just noted). There has been a growing intellectual acceptance, even in some business circles, that the rate of economic growth cannot and should not be sustained at past levels; at the same time, we are reluctant to explore the significance of this conclusion.

But one consequence seems unavoidable. If growth can no longer be counted on to provide for all the major wants, private and public, of a society, or to sustain all the peripheral members of a society at a level that keeps a lid on mutinous outbreaks, especially in congested urban centers, then *some* specification of a nation's most serious needs—its social priorities—and *some* direction as to how goods are to be allocated among society's members are needed. The appropriate word is *planning*. Planning may be comprehensive or piecemeal, compulsory or advisory, long-run or short-run, but whatever its form, planning means identifying priorities in the production and distribution of economic resources. It is here that political decisionmaking challenges the autonomous corporation.

It was easier in an earlier day to support individualism, including economic discretion, as the expression of a more basic philosophical freedom. But in our times—in the process of change from pastoral society to massive industrialism, from small-scale, open settlements to large, packaged populations, from amateur experimentation with keys on kites to scientific applications having major impact far from their source, with populations pressing hard on resources and resorting to modern forms of massed political power to cut themselves into the distribution of consumer goods—the autonomous corporation, free as an individual in its business decisions, has become an anachronism. A philosophy of privatism that extends to the large business corporation is no longer tenable.

Corporate managers who bitterly assail the accumulating federal regulations with which they must cope contend, and with vehemence, that they have long since lost their privacy, at least since the New Deal.

> The heavily individualistic tenor of *caveat emptor* has been largely supplanted by a myriad of class-oriented consumer protection laws, and employment relations, which once were a matter of individual agreement between master and servant, have been circumscribed by regulations setting minimum wages, prescribing safety and health regulations, and prohibiting discrimination based on race, sex, age, creed, and national origin as Congress has moved to protect consumers, workers, and minorities as classes.[11]

But such protective legislation still accepts the basic premise of corporate autonomy. The legislation provides a framework within which the business firm can operate as it chooses or cease to operate if it chooses. The burden of governmental regulation has grown phenomenally in response to social pressures, proscribing certain corporate conduct but without modifying corporate objective. The difference was noted by David Rockefeller, chairman of the board of Chase Manhattan Bank: "Today, society's heightened expectations of an improved life are increasingly coming to bear upon private institutions, as well as traditional public institutions. Major corporations are being asked not merely to support, but to help devise and carry out basic strategies to eliminate social ills."[12] The Committee for Economic Development (CED), a businessman's organization, came to much the same conclusion. Maintaining that society increasingly turns to business corporations for help in solving major problems, CED explained: "Out of a mixture of public frustration and respect for the perceived efficiency of business organizations, there is a clear tendency to look to corporations to take up the slack resulting from inadequate performance of other institutions, notably government." For whatever reasons, "broadened expectations of business have been building up for some time."

> Today it is clear that the terms of the contract between society and business are, in fact, changing in substantial and important ways. Business is being asked to assume broader responsibilities to society than ever before and to serve a wider range of human values. Business enterprises, in effect, are being asked to contribute more to the quality of American life than just supplying quantities of goods and services. Inasmuch as business exists to serve society, its future will depend on the quality of management's response to the changing expectations of the public.[13]

Given their autonomy, corporations even within a regulatory framework are structured to realize profits efficiently. If this autonomy is called into question—not just through a redrafting of the regulatory contours but through a public sharing in the definition of objectives—profit efficiency, however much leavened by enlightened public relations, can no longer claim to be the singular corporate strategy. It is not so much unchecked corporate power or adverse consequences of corporate power that are at issue but the appropriate uses of corporate power, particularly with respect to major social objectives that can be presumed, on the strength of an evolving political philosophy, to take precedence over individual desires.

Public and Private Purpose

The question of society's right to override private discretion goes back to earlier attempts at social legislation—minimum wages, maximum hours, child labor restrictions, for example—in a day when individualism and voluntarism were considered the bedrock of western democracy and the U.S. Supreme Court could assert that to strike down such inhibiting legislation was not to destroy the public good but to exalt it. That issue, involving the police powers of the state, has for some time been resolved in favor of the state. The point now being raised is different. Concern has shifted from the restraint of actions the corporation *might* have initiated if its privacy had been unchecked; now the focus is on the definition of actions the corporation *actually* undertakes or *could* undertake if corporate decisions were determined by criteria that the corporation *left to itself* would not choose to follow.

The distinction can be seen when applied to America's premier industry, the automobile industry. Left to their own devices the auto manufacturers' objective would be to sell as many cars as they profitably could within whatever regulatory framework involving safety, pollution control, and gasoline conservation Congress might erect. The more cars the better. But if their objective were set in the light of social desiderata, Detroit might become involved in a vigorous effort to *reduce* the population of automobiles by developing alternative means of transportation that would satisfy public needs at lower social costs, even if the profit potential were less.

11

Many leaders in the corporate world have testified that large corporations are in fact being pushed to adopt new strategies involving social purpose. As the CED commented, "The evidence strongly suggests that these are solid and durable trends, not momentary frustrations or fads, and that they are likely to increase rather than diminish in the future."[14]

A New Strategy, A New Structure

Nevertheless, support for new strategies will remain largely wind and words unless there are changes in the structure of the corporation to facilitate them. That proposition has been effectively elaborated by Alfred Chandler, Jr., in *Strategy and Structure: Chapters in the History of Industrial Enterprise*.[15] Concerned with the growth of the contemporary corporation, he concluded from a detailed examination of the period prior to World War II that changes in opportunities and needs from one period to a succeeding period dictated shifts in corporate strategy. And "there seems to be no question that a new strategy created new administrative needs."[16] Delays in developing new institutional devices perhaps reflected executive preoccupation with day-to-day affairs or failure to recognize the organizational problems impeding the success of a new strategy. Resistance to change may also have stemmed from perceived threats to the executive's own organizational or psychological security. In any event, sooner or later the needed structural change had to be forthcoming if the enterprise were to pursue the new strategy efficiently. In the period Chandler examined, new strategies were necessitated chiefly by changes in population, national income, and technology—conditions over which the individual corporation had no control but to which the corporation was obliged to adapt.

Here is where the corporation is challenged today. The changes that are compelling a new corporate strategy are to some extent a continuation of past changes on a vastly altered scale. In part they represent shifts that are more political and social than economic. In total, they demand a new corporate strategy geared to broader objectives than profit and to more specific objectives than whatever production can turn a profit. Profit is not excluded as a goal, but it is no longer exclusive.

Such a changed strategy cannot be pursued effectively without altering the corporate structure. To pretend that social purpose can simply be grafted onto the existing corporate organization is an illusion and an evasion. However, to revise the present corporate structure will not be easy: today's corporate form matured in the permissive atmosphere of the last century, when the principle of corporate privatism replaced the guiding principle of public service. Introducing social purpose depends not only on modifying the internal corporate structure but on reordering working relationships among corporations, other interest groups, and government.

Notes

1. Stuart Bruchey, "Corporation: Historical Development," in Alfred D. Chandler, Jr., Stuart Bruchey, and Louis Galambos (eds.), *The Changing Economic Order* (New York: Harcourt, 1968), p. 143.
2. John P. Davis, *Corporations* (New York: Capricorn, 1961; first published 1904), vol. II, p. 269.
3. Oscar Handlin, with Mary Flug Handlin, "Origins of the American Business Corporation," *Journal of Economic History* 5 (1945):22.
4. Davis, *Corporations*, p. 269.
5. *Business Week*, January 16, 1978, p. 55.
6. *Wall Street Journal*, May 22, 1979.
7. *United States v. Dotterweich*, 320 U.S. 277, 280 (1943), cited in *United States v. Park*, 421 U.S. 658 (1975).
8. Leo Marx, *The Machine in the Garden* (New York: Oxford University Press, 1964, 1976; citations from latter).
9. Ibid., p. 365.
10. *The Economist*, August 18, 1979, p. 34.
11. O. Lee Reed, Jr., "Comments: The Sunshine Society and the Legal Regulation of Business through Compulsory Disclosure," *American Business Law Journal* 16 (Spring 1978): 87.
12. David Rockefeller, "Corporate Capacity for Public Responsibility," *Business Lawyer* 28 (March 1973):55.
13. Committee for Economic Development, *Social Responsibilities of Business Corporations* (New York: CED, 1971), p. 16.
14. *Ibid.*
15. Alfred D. Chandler, Jr., *Strategy and Structure: Chapters in the History of the Industrial Enterprise* (Cambridge: M.I.T. Press, 1962).
16. Ibid., p. 14.

2

Alternatives to Structural Change

Management Ethics

In view of the difficulties of effecting structural change, other methods have been suggested by which the corporation may generate a satisfactory social strategy. One theme that has been widely discussed is the cultivation of management's ethical sensitivity. Periodical publications dealing with business ethics have sprouted; centers for research on business ethics have been endowed; schools of business administration have added courses and seminars on the subject; and numerous corporations have themselves issued codes of ethical conduct for their employees.

Just what "ethical" comprehends is seldom made clear, and even less often is there agreement among those who do define the term. For our purposes ethical conduct means what is right and moral even if such action is neither expected nor required or some *other* course of action is expected or required. Hence, choice among alternatives is necessary before ethics are called into question. Ethical action is based on criteria that seek to create a sense of harmony between the individual and identifiable others whom the individual affects or could affect and between the individual and some con-

14

ceived higher order or authority, which may be deistic, humanistic, or naturalistic. There is often sufficient ambiguity about correct actions to create a basis for criticism and penalty by those contrary-minded; more significant, however, there is likelihood of approval or at least understanding by a large majority of the relevant population. Such approval validates the ethical nature of the choice. Ethical actions are, in short, other-regarding rather than self-regarding, guided by a standard that is not idiosyncratic but widely shared. In the words of the philosopher Paul Carus, "All subjective ethical theories fail to see the cardinal point of ethics, for the very nature of ethics is objective. If there is no objective authority for moral conduct, we had better openly declare that ethics is an illusion."[1] If *anything* goes, what happens to the idea of a *standard* of ethical conduct?

One difficulty with many contemporary attempts at ethics building is that they fail to identify the objective authority that validates ethical behavior. An outstanding exception was provided by the late Carl Madden, for many years chief economist with the U.S. Chamber of Commerce.[2] Madden set out to describe a general cultural standard capable of guiding managers in making choices. In western society the higher authority most broadly accepted is science and the search for truth and dissemination of knowledge that science engenders. Individual ethical behavior must be tested against the demands of this authority. The liberal political system, individualistic and free-thinking, has been the appropriate social system to further this scientific search for truth, allowing inquiry to proceed in any direction. The competitive market system has been the instrument for the practical application of scientific discoveries.

But as the institutionalized corporation evolved out of the liberal market system, the objective ethical standard has been undermined. The corporate individual becomes subordinated to the demands of the corporation, which are to get out and win by almost any expedient. The competitive, individualistic spirit becomes a team spirit, its objective to advance the corporation, the individual player evaluated and rewarded on the basis of his team performance. Corporate aggrandizement—the drive for a target rate of return or market share—overrides the general ethic of truth seeking and truth telling.

Madden did not burden his essay with the supporting detail that can be culled from almost any newspaper or news magazine, nor is it necessary here to do more than mention such examples as false advertising, adulteration or premature marketing of products (sometimes jeopardizing health or safety), falsification of records for government inspectors, and refusal to confront the probable health hazards of certain work settings.

Can managers be ethical individuals within a corporation and retain their positions? If not, as Madden believed, then an objective ethical standard, even though generally accepted within western society, cannot be relied on to guide corporate behavior. To the contrary, the organizational imperative requires the corporate employee to shape his behavior to the wanted results if he desires to remain with the organization.

There is, however, more to the problem than organizational cupidity. Organizations—especially those of the size and functional importance of large corporations—cannot escape the exercise of power. But ethics ignore the issues of organized power. Even so-called scientific truth carries no answer as to the appropriate uses of such truth. That is a political matter, not the privileged choice of an individual. Decisions of this nature involve negotiation and compromise among people in power in order to accommodate differing perceptions of subordinates and colleagues and thereby to hold the organization together. And compromise in policy matters means juggling both the decisionmakers' and others' conceptions and preferred uses of truth—others being both in the organization (staff) and outside (customers, dealers, suppliers, regulators). The use of power in organizational policymaking requires the sacrifice of a personal ethical guide, at least in matters of importance. Jean-Jacques Rousseau put the matter precisely: "However truthful a man may be, he must lie sometimes if he is a bishop."[3]

The implementation of an appropriate social strategy for the modern corporation cannot be achieved simply by relying on the ethical probity of managers. The organization has its own demands, taking precedence over the views of individual members.

Corporate Social Responsibility

Even if the organization takes precedence over the individual, is it not possible to develop within the existing structure a *corporate* social strategy that accomplishes desired results by processes already familiar to the organization? After all, production, marketing, and financial policies must all be fashioned from the often divergent views of the management corps. Why not social policy as well?

John deButts, chief executive officer of American Telephone and Telegraph, is one of numerous corporate leaders who believe that such a result is not only feasible but is already being realized, even if imperfectly:

> Whether a business has social responsibilities is, I know, a subject of widespread debate. But to my mind, it is a debate that continues long after the argument is over. Today I know of no leader of business who sees his function as limited to the pursuit of profit. I know of none who does not realize that the business that for profit's sake ignores the impacts of its actions on society is not likely to make a profit very long. In short, it has come to be widely recognized that to focus strategic planning activities on market opportunities alone is insufficient and may, in fact, be counterproductive.[4]

The strategic planning needed to accomplish the objective "must be integrated with the on-going processes of management." DeButts identified five "basic ingredients":

1. knowledge of constituent demands,
2. an understanding of environmental trends,
3. a method of integrating and analyzing that knowledge and understanding,
4. effective internal communications, and
5. individual accountability of managers.[5]

Strategic planning is one of the most recent and most favored additions to the portfolio of managerial techniques. While this approach calls for organizational changes internal to the corporation, they are the kind of changes that companies are used to making, such as the addition of a new office or department, a shift to decentralized management or a tightening of central control (perhaps in response to new government regulations, as with respect to bribery), or an alteration in the internal communications process. But these examples differ from the kind of structural change that redirects the corporation to perform in ways that otherwise would not have been *possible*. DeButts clearly noted this difference though he found it inapplicable:

> Always in a dynamic society there are mismatches between traditional institutional arrangements and current realities. Currently

> there is a mismatch between traditional corporate forms and processes and the demands of the corporation's new constituencies. Some argue that this mismatch is so great that only fundamental restructuring of the rules of corporate governance will suffice to close it. I do not agree.[6]

Thus, for deButts, a new strategy embracing public purpose would involve a change in performance that could be accomplished without the corporation's breaking stride, that is, simply by impressing a few new rules and procedures on the people in authority.

Earl Cheit has presented a more sophisticated version of deButts's thesis.[7] Cheit recognized the reality of corporate power in society and he largely accepted the attenuation of ownership control over management—the latter's self-selection via proxy machinery in conjunction with a large, dispersed stockholder constituency. The issue, then, becomes one of justifying this assumption of power in a democratic society. If the modern corporation exercises an influence comparable to the church's in medieval society, as some have contended, that authority cannot be said to enjoy the same legitimacy. If corporate management is largely self-selected, who or what sanctions its actions? Some accountability is called for.

Cheit weaves a subtle response. First, the degree of power accruing to the management of any single corporation is circumscribed. For all its size, the corporation operates in a competitive world that shows little mercy. The competition may come from other corporations in the same industry, from companies providing alternative products that are cheaper or technologically superior, or from foreign corporations. Managers are kept on their toes to perform satisfactorily in this environment. But if competition is so severe, what room is there for even the giants to depart from the discipline of the balance sheet by engaging in socially responsive actions that do not contribute to profit?

In addition to facing stiff competition, Cheit continues, managers face a fluid social context. The public, sometimes persuaded by the activities of public-interest defenders, is quick to condemn corporate behavior viewed as antisocial. The corporation thus ignores at its peril external demands being made. Pressures may build to the point of eliciting government regulations more costly to meet than independent corporate efforts to correct the targeted problem would have been to complete. Corporate social responsibility can thus be "best understood as part of the process of absorbing the impact of this changing environment."[8] The goals internal to the firm are modified by outside influences.

Cheit's image of the modern corporation corresponds to David Riesman's conception of the "other-directed" man.[9] The corporate public affairs department no longer simply paints an attractive public face for the private profit-seeking enterprise. It hoists its own antenna to pick up whatever signals the public is sending its way, and the enterprise bends itself to those signals to preserve credibility and acceptability. The self-made (inner directed) entrepreneur of an earlier day has given way to the politically responsive (public influenced) corporate government of today. Cheit's process of absorbing the impact of the changing environment corresponds to deButts's strategic planning toward this end: "When the environment changes and the organization no longer fits, its listening devices report the change. If the organization is to survive over a long period, it must make the necessary alterations in its behavior. These changes, in turn, influence the environment and set in motion a continuing chain of adjustments until a satisfactory fit is achieved."[10] Paul Samuelson rounded out the picture: "The several hundred large corporations react to, and set, an evolving code of social conduct. So long as anyone does not depart too markedly from the ruling norm, it will not be penalized out of existence by market competition."[11]

For all the plausibility of this portrait of the large corporation, zealously guarding capital investments by measuring up to what the public wants from it not only in terms of products and prices but also in terms of social programs, the picture seems bland. The image of a smooth-faced, corporate eunuch, conscientiously performing a neutral role, doing wisely and cheerfully what is asked, hardly is the view most of us have of the large, target oriented, hard-driving, budget constrained institution we know as the modern corporation. Does business have no special interests of its own that are deeply rooted in the organizational psyche and that it strives to achieve against all obstacles—including a critical public? Does business simply react to public opinion—or does it seek to mold that opinion in its own interests? When the public relations department, with all its present sophistication, hoists its antenna to hear what is being said, does it sometimes get back signals it sent out itself?

David Linowes, a businessman and public accountant, observed that managers attempt equally to fashion and to respond to their environment: "Big corporations, in their profit pursuits and at times outside their profit pursuits, act aggressively to shape and influence the laws they virtuously conform to."[12] Robert Heilbroner concluded that however much corporate managers may survey the changing social scene, their scanning discovers nothing calling for significant departures from existing social arrangements. Whatever signals their antennas may pick up are conservatively interpreted and responded to; what is lacking is "a projection of human possibilities cast in a larger mold than is offered by today's institutions."[13] Thus, Linowes and Heilbroner doubly indicted the deButts-Cheit thesis: not only is there missing an understanding of the need for structural change if a new social strategy is to be realized but the "new" corporate social strategy is so undemanding that it does not require an altered structure. A prominent lawyer put the matter bluntly:

> Despite the apparent inclination of many business managers today to march under a banner of "social responsibility," the debate over the corporate social role will no doubt remain because our economic model continues to generate pressure *against* effective social action by corporations—except on the *token* scale. Under the system of private capital freely employed, subject to the invisible hand of market incentives—essentially a system of decision-making by the individual company—it may be inevitable that social costs and environmental disruption are by-products of profits and growth. We should recognize that the individual company will always be expected to strain to reduce *its* costs by shifting to others—*i.e.*, to society—whatever costs can be lodged there.[14]

If social responsibility remains a discretionary power of corporate management, the central objective of the corporation will remain its rate of return, however constrained by fear of adverse public sentiment if the corporation carries that objective too far. If the desired change in corporate strategy is not simply to inculcate in present managers a greater sensitivity to the way profit is pursued, if the strategy needed is one that uses the corporation for social purposes that incorporate but transcend profit, then an attitude of social responsibility is no reliable alternative to a change in organizational structure.

The Ethical Investor

The social—chiefly student—agitation of the late 1960s focused on the failure of institutions to perform in socially desirable ways and promoted greater participation in institutional decisionmaking. In this climate university campuses witnessed the creation of senates in which administration, faculty, and students could jointly seek to resolve divisive issues. At the same time, the corporate arena invited the conclusion that corporate sins should not be charged solely to management but also to stockholders—the public owners of the corporation should accept a moral responsibility to mend the corporation's ways.

This idea was elaborated with considerable sophistication in a number of publications. If the phrase "ethical investor" had been intended to imply that the individual stockholder should correspond with his company or vote on resolutions contained in the proxy statement, the term would have raised some of the issues pertaining to the ethical manager examined earlier, except that the stockholder would be all the less effective for being on the periphery of the action. No hope here for corporate reformation. In fact, the ethical investor who counted was itself an institution—a university, a church, a pension fund, even a municipality. These entities controlled blocks of stocks large enough to justify and, in the thinking of the day, to require the holders' involvement. Moreover, when Yale University took a position on some General Motors policy, its name counted more than its number of shares. The hope behind the ethical investor movement, then, was that people like churchmen and educators in leadership roles were less conservative, more idealistic, in their conception of the good society and the contribution a corporation might make thereto: with enough institutional representatives active, management would have to pay attention; thus, the corporation would necessarily become more conscious of and responsive to social issues even while pursuing profit.

A meeting of representatives of interested institutions to discuss procedures for making such a strategy effective revealed an interesting difference of views. The principal issue centered on whether the institutional investor should adopt a set of criteria to guide its officers in taking a stance with respect to specific actions of corporations in which they held shares or whether the institution should rely on the judgment—"intuitive integrity" was the term employed —of its officers, which presumably would reflect their understanding of the ethical concerns of their own constituency. The argument on behalf of specified criteria was that they would help the representative of the shareholding institution articulate a defensible position. As one conference participant noted:

21

> I am worried about simply allowing intuitive integrity to operate untrammeled by criteria. If as a trustee you have no criteria at all, you may well start thinking about what might be the effects of an action. All kinds of things may come floating before your mind as potential consequences which could damage the institution. Criteria help you organize the relative weights to be given to these considerations.[15]

The opposing camp held that criteria "tend to suggest a precision that is altogether missing in any of the issues that are at all difficult; and . . . if they are not difficult, you don't need much in the way of criteria to handle them."[16]

A secondary issue was whether the position and priorities of the ethical investor varied with its constituency's special interests. A women's college might perhaps be more concerned about equal employment opportunities in business, while a religious body might focus more on the morality of encouraging sales of sweets and soft drinks to low-income populations suffering from malnutrition. Again, there were pros and cons. A participant explained: "Either I think in some fundamental way that discriminating against women in upward mobility and employment opportunities is wrong and that this is a wrong that should be corrected, or else I think that it is something trivial and unimportant that institutional investors ought just to forget about." Another replied:

> It seems to me that what you do as a member of a church board should really be quite different from what you do for Yale University. If you take a social view which has gotten clarified in your church context, or has become part of your conscience, and as a university trustee use it to begin to push corporations around, you are bound . . . to put a lot of professors and a lot of students in very strange kinds of positions.[17]

Practically, the philosophy of ethical investing seems more attuned to massaging the conscience of the investor through taking stands than to affecting the corporation's vision of its objectives. However brave the intention, the mechanism is weak. Large corporations engage in activities on so many fronts that no investor—however institutionalized or ethical—can hope to monitor them all. Even though research organizations have come into existence to assist in the monitoring function, there remains the problem of "netting out" the company's performance. Does investment in South Africa counterbalance a good job training program for inner city minorities at home? Beyond the problem of the multiplicity of corporate actions that somehow add up to corporate purpose lies the more intractable difficulty that the ethical investor is always running after the train. Even if corporate management responds affirmatively to the shareholder's ethical position, the *basic* corporate strategy has changed not a whit. New issues will be raised again and again, and the same management will respond to them impelled by the same, unchanged institutionalized drive, however much that management may keep in mind how some church or university shareholder may view the outcome.

The fundamental corporate strategy remains firmly in place, simply applied with greater consideration for more sensitive consciences. This tactic does nothing but create a minor detour on the road the corporation is traveling to its own destination, a target rate of return.

Industrywide Collaboration

If competition directs the corporation toward an almost singular goal of profit performance within social constraints, could a collaborative, industrywide effort lessen the competitive push and encourage the pursuit of multiple objectives? The question itself suggests one major difficulty. Any arrangement that lessens competitive pressure on the individual corporation is as likely to jeopardize consumer interests (by allowing concerted action to maintain price or cheapen quality) as to further the public interest (by permitting joint action for broader aims than a corporation's own rate of return). While present antitrust legislation may be considered protection against combinations following the former course, such protection would almost certainly have to be sacrificed to allow any effective version of the second course of action.

One answer to the dilemma is vaguely reassuring. A few corporate giants dominate many industries today; thus, concerted effort is now possible despite antitrust legislation. Price competition can be restrained by a process of quasi-bargaining, in which—without direct contact—companies forego significant price actions, to increase either market share (through price cutting) or profit (through price hikes), that are not likely to be endorsed industrywide. Through mutual understanding gained from years of experience they know, without the need for formal agreement, the

23

narrow limits within which they can engage in price competition without inviting reprisal.[18] These limits are rarely transgressed. When price actions are needed because of altered circumstances—either a raising or a lowering of prices—the move can be coordinated by judicious, overt, and perfectly legal signals exchanged among the corporations (as, for example, by testing both public and industry opinion through press conferences). Under such circumstances, more formal industrywide collaboration may carry little more threat to consumer welfare than already exists, while at least a potential for good might be realized. Business firms already enjoying a degree of joint market control might, for example, be led to exercise discretion in the old guild manner of maintaining industry honor through such public service as policing quality standards; a crasser motivation might be to avoid government regulations by instituting self-regulation.

The advertising industry has over the years, and especially since 1971, undertaken several forms of self-regulation, including use of outsiders, in a continuing effort to reduce public criticism of objectionable advertising. A more recent attempt to placate the public has been made by the nuclear branch of the utility industry. Following the costly accident at General Public Utilities Corporation's Three Mile Island plant in Pennsylvania, with its attendant worldwide publicity, an Institute of Nuclear Power Operations was established. Among its projected responsibilities were improved operator training and emergency management plus a periodic audit and evaluation of the safety programs of nuclear plants, the latter to be required as a condition for participating in an industry insurance pool. In the words of one utility official, "It became imperative that we do whatever is necessary as an industry to see that [the Three Mile Island accident] does not happen again."[19]

There are serious limitations on this self-regulatory approach to public-interest objectives. "Programs that are weak and ineffectual run the danger of merely forestalling for a time the introduction of some more fundamental outside remedy,"[20] but programs that are strong enough to be effective may deter corporations from participating. In the case of the nuclear power industry the dilemma of too weak or too strong was linked by one expert to the potential success of the strategy in preserving industry autonomy. If the industry were to win public credibility, it would almost of necessity have to issue some reports critical of corporate performance; not to do so would suggest that it had set standards too low to be of value. But if any negative reports were issued in so sensitive a field, they could be expected to stir up public demand for stronger government regulation.[21]

From the perspective of the present study, a more serious reservation to industry self-regulation is that this approach would focus largely on remedial or maintenance measures. A code of conduct is unlikely to provide a base for innovative social use of the private corporation. This latter objective could be achieved by industry programs specifically designed not to regulate but to stimulate new actions of a public-interest nature on the part of corporate members. The life insurance industry undertook such an effort in 1967. Following the racial riots that broke out in most American inner cities, the Life Insurance Association of America pledged, on the part of its members, $1 billion to improve housing and employment in the nation's urban slums (the amount was subsequently raised to $2 billion). The pledge was heavily publicized, the initial announcement coming from the office of the president of the United States.

Political scientist Karen Orren studied the results of this program, specifically in Illinois, a leading state in the volume of life insurance assets domiciled there.[22] Orren's conclusions, to the extent they can be applied to other industries, as appears probable, were bleak. The instincts of the industry—its basic drives—pointed to two overriding objectives: profits and autonomy. The Urban Investments Program, aimed chiefly at the latter goal, sought to ward off government limitations on discretion in selecting investment opportunities (so-called red-lining). But the same reluctance to share discretion that the industry showed vis-a-vis the government, each corporate member displayed with respect to fellow members of the industry.

Each company was guided by its own criteria. Since the chief among these had, in the past, been profit performance, each company—out of the experience built into its operations—continued to follow the same guide even if it attempted, at the same time, to eliminate any racial prejudice that had intruded into its past decisions. And "when in the Urban Investments Program an effort was made to cleanse investment procedures of racial bias without imposing any specific new goals, the habits of underwriting channeled funds straight to the most profitable or peripheral segments of the ghetto community, most of which were already served adequately in financial markets."[23] Hence, the presumed goal of revitalizing the inner cities lacked substance.

The individual corporation's tenacious defense of its own autonomy thus would seem to make concerted industry action an unlikely vehicle for broader programs. Granted that for such concerted action to be successful some relaxation of antitrust legislation would be necessary, the evidence suggests that by itself this strategy would not be sufficient. To develop programs with a different social vision requires an *industry strategy*, which is to say an abandonment of corporate autonomy. Moreover, simply to achieve the collaborative and cumulative effects intended, a new *industry structure*, affecting each constituent corporate member, is needed, which takes us back to my initial thesis.

To conclude, voluntary concerted action on an industrywide basis is no alternative to novel organizational forms. The public-interest or self-regulatory approach is limited largely to policing socially injurious actions on the part of industry members; it does not pretend to significant new initiatives. Concerted industry action on behalf of new social goals is frustrated in the first instance by the strong predilection for autonomy among corporations. Should that tendency be overcome, we would see more clearly than ever the need for a revised institutional structure.

Government Regulation

If self-regulation by industry tends to be preventive and remedial rather than innovative, the same can be said of much governmental regulation of industry. Consumer health and safety, occupational safeguards, environmental protection, truth in advertising, full disclosure in the sale of securities—these and many other legal requirements deal with flaws (potential or actual) in present corporate practice. But government regulation does at times initiate changes in corporate behavior significant enough to produce major·alterations in the social system. The National Labor Relations Act of 1935, for example, in regulating industrial relations transformed the character of the workplace for millions of Americans.

What remains true, despite such exceptions, is that government is geared to incremental changes in an existing and dense network of corporate actions, so that the design of the whole is little affected by any single intervention. Government regulation builds piece on piece, in an ad hoc manner, with little concern either for the relationship of one piece to another or for the total impact. It is unlikely

26

that such piecemeal actions will generate corporate behavior tending toward more creative social programs. Indeed, virtually all ideological quarters have testified that the cumulative effect of increasing government regulation is to hobble corporations in performing their traditional social roles of production and distribution. Each piece of legislation and each provision of every law has its defenders (sometimes including the affected corporations, which may find government requirements a welcome barrier to competition), but there is no practical procedure for screening out, or even measuring the effects of, provisions or laws that—however desirable when considered separately—give rise to a loss of social advantage rather than a gain when added to the body of other regulations.

There are many ways, of course, that people in so-called nonproductive jobs can add to the quality of life for everyone, something as true of government bureaucracies (including regulators) as of corporate bureaucracies. On the other hand, the weight of such social overhead may in time mean a poorer quality of life. As *The Economist* remarked of Britain's civil service: "Among these are a lot of intelligent people without enough to do. They therefore manufacture government activity, do endless hypothetical or contingency work (most of it never used), produce a mass of long-term planning (which is almost always overtaken by events), strive to an extravagant approximation of perfection and accuracy, or simply shuffle paper."[24] While this sort of criticism has often come from people opposed to any sort of social change, it is now also being voiced by people who believe that social change is not proceeding fast enough.

The administration and enforcement of most regulatory laws depend on the firms that are themselves being regulated. Under the Consumer Products Safety Act, a manufacturer, wholesaler, distributor, or retailer must report within twenty-four hours the discovery of any "substantial" hazard in a product (what is substantial is a matter for the company to decide). Pharmaceutical firms must report unexpected effects of new drugs to the Food and Drug Administration. Ship operators must report oil spills. Automobile manufacturers must report test results on exhaust emissions. The Water Pollution Control Act requires reports on any failure of pollution controls. As an official of the Environmental Protection Agency remarked, on an occasion when Olin executives discovered that internal company reports concerning waste discharges had been falsified (and thereupon notified EPA): "Self-policing is the whole cornerstone of the Water Pollution Control Act." Another agency staff member added: "There is no other way to administer a law that covers so many people. . . . it would require a police state and a huge bureaucracy."[25]

Given the number and complexity of regulatory provisions affecting most large corporations, American managers have done a creditable job in performing the self-policing mandated by government. Nevertheless, there are grounds for questioning whether, as the regulatory requirements continue to mount, actual compliance may not be a haphazard matter. Christopher Stone, professor of law at the University of Southern California, is clearly of that opinion. Stone catalogued a number of reasons why conformance with legal requirements may not rank high on a company's list of priorities.[26] Of the many risks to profit performance, a fine for infraction of some regulatory provision is likely to be relatively inconsequential. The uncertainty of any governmental check for compliance further lessens the risk. Aside from such pragmatic considerations, the number and complexity of legal regulations make infraction of some law almost inevitable—hence less of a cause for any sense of corporate shame or guilt (how many large corporations do not have antitrust charges pending?). The vague wording of some laws and the range of possible interpretations leave compliance a relative rather than a precise matter. For many operating managers, immediate objectives of output or sales (built into quotas and budgets) govern their behavior, not the remote prospect of penalty for the infraction of rules they may not even respect; sometimes, willful infractions at lower levels are screened out of reports made to superiors, both to avoid exposure of persons directly involved and to protect people in positions of higher responsibility from the culpability that comes with knowledge of unreported wrongdoing.

A former EPA administrator, Russell Train, also questioned the adequacy of corporate self-enforcement of government regulations: "It is not practical to believe that industry will police itself. And that is not to be critical. Many elements of industry are very responsible. But industry is a very big name. This would be like saying, 'Do you think it's reasonable to expect society to fully police itself?' The answer is no."[27]

In some areas—notably pollution control and resource use—economists have recommended that the pricing mechanism be substituted for regulation. Effluent charges, for example, could be imposed on a company dumping industrial wastes into a river or lake. This policy would raise production costs, reflected in higher product prices, reducing the output of goods whose adjusted prices would mirror real costs ("internalizing social costs" is the descriptive term) or encouraging the producer to improve technology and reduce wastes. In either event, the market would do the job of regulation, dispensing with bureaucratic interventions.

The move to incorporate the social impact of private enterprise into business accounting has an intuitive appeal but carries grave problems. The question of measuring social costs is obviously thorny though perhaps manageable if we are satisfied with less than logical perfection. More seriously, unless this is to be simply another ad hoc legislative maneuver, government would have to take a series of related measures. If all enterprises internalized all social costs, which were then reflected in higher prices, the cost of living (measured by some market basket of goods) would rise to levels beyond the reach of marginal income groups. Food, housing, and clothing—not to mention amenities like television and automobiles— would become more costly. Subsidies would have to be provided to low-income groups to compensate for the hardship of higher prices on certain consumer necessities—a difficulty recognized but underestimated by pricing mechanism advocates. If effluent charges failed either to stem waste output or to encourage new technology, the charges would have to be manipulated (what else would this be but a form of regulation?) or explicit controls would have to be reinstated. The most serious deficiency of internalized costing is that this strategy would operate only on the negative by-product of economic activity, ignoring the potential for using the large enterprise affirmatively for social purposes.

Despite the limitations of the device, one can readily sympathize with the intent to incorporate a proven motivation into the procurement of a desired social result. The President's Commission on the Accident at Three Mile Island noted the deadening effect of regulation without motivation: "The existence of a vast body of regulations by [the Nuclear Regulatory Commission] tends to focus industry attention narrowly on the meeting of regulations rather than on a systematic concern for safety."[28] James Crary, a student of both psychology and business, commented:

> Once the novelty of being watched has passed, there is nothing to prevent a corporation from developing an immunity, despite the most virulent regulatory presence. Involved here is not the resis-

tive evil intent of business, but the simple notion that business interests have not been well incorporated into the work flow or the administrative protocol. If the limits of corporate responsibility and the limits of regulation have been reached, what is the next step?[29]

In spite of all the criticisms that have been leveled against excesses, there is no way to avoid government regulation of industry. That point is not at issue. At best society can find ways of reducing the burden of such regulation. But for purposes of the present exploration, the fundamental consideration is that by itself regulation, like the internalizing of social costs, does not constitute a corporate social strategy integrating vision, motivation, and discretion and in the long run can make the creation of such a strategy and its facilitating structure all the more difficult and uncertain.

Notes

1. Paul Carus, *The History of the Devil and the Idea of Evil* (New York: Bell, 1969), p. 457.
2. Carl Madden, "Forces Which Influence Ethical Behavior," in Clarence C. Walton (ed.), *The Ethics of Corporate Conduct* (Englewood Cliffs: Prentice-Hall, 1977), pp. 31–78.
3. Jean-Jacques Rousseau, *The Confessions* (Baltimore: Penguin, 1954), p. 218.
4. John D. deButts, "A Strategy of Accountability," in William R. Dill (ed.), *Running the American Corporation* (Englewood Cliffs: Prentice-Hall, 1978), p. 146.
5. Ibid., p. 147.
6. Ibid., p. 152.
7. Earl F. Cheit, "The New Place of Business: Why Managers Cultivate Social Responsibility," in Earl F. Cheit (ed.), *The Business Establishment* (New York: Wiley, 1964), pp. 152–192.
8. Ibid., p. 188.
9. David Riesman and Nathan Glazer, *The Lonely Crowd* (New Haven: Yale University Press, 1951).
10. Cheit, "The New Place of Business," p. 190.
11. Paul A. Samuelson, "Love That Corporation," *New York Times*, December 26, 1970.
12. David Linowes, *The Corporate Conscience* (New York: Hawthorn, 1974), p. 25.
13. Robert L. Heilbroner, "The View from the Top: Reflections on a Changing Business Ideology," in Cheit, *The Business Establishment*, p. 35.

14. Bevis Longstreth in a panel discussion, "Corporate Responsibility Panel: The Role of the SEC," *Business Lawyer* 28 (March 1973): 224–225.
15. Charles W. Powers (ed.), *People/Profits: The Ethics of Investment* (New York: Council on Religion and International Affairs, 1972), p. 101.
16. Ibid., p. 103.
17. Ibid., p. 100.
18. This relationship was most fully explored by William J. Fellner in *Competition among the Few* (New York: Knopf, 1949).
19. *Business Week*, September 17, 1979, p. 35.
20. Harvey Levin, "The Limits of Self-regulation," *Columbia Law Review* 67 (April 1967): 605.
21. *Business Week*, September 17, 1979, p. 36.
22. Karen Orren, *Corporate Power and Social Change* (Baltimore: Johns Hopkins Press, 1974).
23. Ibid., pp. 182–183.
24. *The Economist*, January 12, 1980, p. 17.
25. *New York Times*, March 25, 1978.
26. Christopher Stone, *Where the Law Ends* (New York: Harper & Row, 1975), pp. 36–46.
27. *New York Times*, March 25, 1978.
28. *New York Times*, October 31, 1979.
29. James Crary, "Ethical Problems in the Interaction of the Systems of Business and Government" (Columbia University Graduate School of Business Seminar in Corporate Relations, August 20, 1979).

3

Proposals for Restructuring the Ultimate Corporate Authority

The board of directors is commonly considered the ultimate authority within the corporation.[1] What role this ultimate authority actually plays is less clear-cut. Melvin Eisenberg observed that while the legal model has the board selecting the corporation's officers, setting corporate policy, and managing the corporation, in fact the board does not and cannot do any of these things. Constraints of time and information make it impossible for any but full-time operating officers to cope with the ongoing strategic and operational activities.[2] Various reports and surveys also suggest that board practice conforms to Eisenberg's judgment. For instance, in a wide-ranging study of medium and large corporations, Myles Mace of the Harvard Business School found that typically boards serve as a source of advice and counsel, as a source—mostly potential or latent—of discipline for company presidents, and as a source of authoritative decisionmaking in times of crisis. They were there to be used in the chief executive's discretion or to be forced into action when he seemed to be floundering. Otherwise, they sit idle: "A few boards establish objectives, strategies, and policies. Most do not. . . . A few boards ask discerning questions of the management. Most do not."[3]

If the board is to serve as the ultimate authority of the corporation—and where else might such authority be placed?—it seems essential that board practice be overhauled. To this end two key issues must be resolved: what should be the board's role; and what changes in its composition and method of functioning are necessary to permit, or perhaps to oblige, it to play this role? So much has been written on this topic that the following review must condense the debate drastically.

The consensus is that boards cannot become involved either in formulating strategic decisions or in making them operational. Nevertheless, there is an apparent reluctance to leave managers in so exposed a position of responsibility. Boards, it is argued, should authorize "major corporate actions"[4] and provide prior "consideration of decisions and actions with a potential for major economic impact."[5] But such involvement in policy is precisely the sort that critics consider boards unable satisfactorily to puruse since the board's reviewing role must normally rely "on analyses prepared by the very executives who formulate that which is being analyzed." Thus, Eisenberg concluded that "aside from the potential check it provides in conflict-of-interest cases, the board's authorization function, like its advice-and-counsel function, is of limited importance."[6]

If we lay aside for the moment the obvious ambivalence concerning the authorization of major corporate policies by the board, virtually all observers agree that the board can successfully evaluate the company's actual performance. This task implies continuous monitoring of management's performance—and readiness to dismiss presidents who are not performing well. In fact, precisely because so much discretion and initiative inhere in the chief executive's office, the choice of chief executive and the ongoing evaluation of his performance can realistically be called the board's principal function.

With this major role, the board must be independent of management. In Christopher Stone's picturesque Freudian analogy, if management is the corporation's id (aggressive and assertive), the board is the corporation's superego, acting as governor over the id —restraining any misguided impulsiveness and promoting appropriate relationships with others in society.[7] People who monitor the chief executive should not themselves (as they usually are now) be dependent on the chief executive for their own nomination to the board and their continuity in office, for the organization and functioning of the board, and for the information on which they rely. How can such a reversal of roles be achieved?

Outside Directors

Inside directors are members of operating management—the president, vice-president, and staff officers who have been placed on the board because of their intimate knowledge of the business. But if the function of management is to manage, this job can best be done off the board. If the function of the board is to select and monitor management, managers should not be expected to sit in judgment on themselves. The conflict of interest is too blunt. Inside directors subordinate to the president in the management structure cannot be expected to appraise him critically and objectively as board members. Moreover, the corporate performance that they are asked to evaluate is presumably one that they have helped to bring about. The limitations of inside directors are so well understood that about the only reasons for using them are their expertise and availability; still, the specialized knowledge they possess can be tapped in questioning before the board.

Outside directors come with no operating responsibility in the business and presumably with no personal interest other than ownership of some shares of stock (usually a small amount, sometimes none). Their contributions are supposedly several. Outsiders who are executives of other companies bring a business capability; they can be expected to know where to look for weaknesses and strengths. Nonbusiness types—professional people such as lawyers and academics—are likely to be more sensitive to the public and internal effects of corporate actions. The lack of personal stake in company policy—the element of objectivity—sometimes has won outside directors a special status with courts and the Securities and Exchange Commission, converting them almost into an arm of the government:

> The [SEC] has come to rely on outside directors to promote some of its own regulatory objectives. In pathological situations where the commission has reached settlements with corporations that have been the subject of commission action, it has required the formation of committees of outside directors, sometimes newly chosen, to direct investigations. . . . After such a committee reports to the full board, it is expected that the board will remedy

34

improper past practices and devise procedures to prevent their re-currence.[8]

The logic of outside—more specifically, independent—directors as opposed to insiders has persuaded some analysts that the board should be composed only of outsiders: "Why is there even a *reason* for insiders to serve on the board?"[9] Courtney Brown, former dean of the Columbia University Graduate School of Business, would in-clude only the chief executive officer.[10] Eisenberg, while inclined to the logic of this position, suggested a compromise: "Despite the ad-vantages of a rule mandating complete independence, a rule re-quiring that only a clear majority of the board be independent would probably be preferable, at least today"; it would avoid "an unacceptably sharp break with tradition."[11] The prestigious Busi-ness Roundtable echoed Eisenberg's opinion, rejecting the all-out-sider board as extreme but viewing "a majority of nonmanagement directors" as desirable.[12]

Outsider status does not guarantee the independence of such di-rectors. Election takes place, at the corporation's annual meeting, by means of shareholder proxies. Nomination of a candidate—his place on the proxy statement—is tantamount to election. If the power to nominate and solicit proxies remains with management, as is now typically the case, management would effectively control the choice of outside directors, a condition scarcely conducive to their independence—hence the widespread agreement among ob-jective observers that outside directors should themselves control the nomination of directors and the proxy machinery: "Only so can the monitoring function be made effective."[13]

Other problems relate to the organization and functioning of the board. As Noyes Leech and Robert Mundheim noted: "The chang-ing responsibilities being imposed on directors . . . can only be ful-filled if accountability rests on institutional procedures rather than on the willingness of an outside director individually to take un-pleasant initiatives at board meetings or otherwise appear to be act-ing in a personally hostile manner." They rejected "ad hoc expedi-ents to enforce accountability sporadically" in favor of more explicit board structure and functions.[14]

The more efficient use of committees has attracted widespread support. Although numerous individuals, including managers, have urged that directors be expected or required to spend more time on corporate affairs, most observers agree that short of having a full-time responsibility the independent director cannot possibly know enough about corporate operation and plans to make informed evaluations or monitor management performance. This limitation can be overcome at least partially by assigning each board member to a committee, charged with specific responsibilities, that reports to the full board. Brown, who has perhaps gone furthest in this direction, suggested that board activity should take place chiefly through committees.[15] Most analysts would provide for nominating, audit, and compensation committees composed wholly or largely of independent directors. The Business Roundtable, for example, accepted complete independence for audit and compensation committees and a majority of outside directors for nominating committees.[16] Since 1978 the New York Stock Exchange has required that all listed companies have an audit committee composed wholly of outsiders. Leech and Mundheim would exact the same requirement of the nominating committee but stipulated that it should consult with the chief executive officer.[17]

When boards include inside directors, some committees, perhaps even the executive committee, may be dominated by members coming from management. This possibility focuses attention on the powers of the chairman of the board, who in addition to making committee assignments also may call board meetings, determine agendas, and preside over meetings—not inconsequential prerogatives. Some have recommended that in boards with mixed memberships an outsider should be named chairman. The independent chairman would be given the responsibility of organizing the board and insuring the freedom of its committees from excessive managerial influence.

Vesting the functions of board chairman in someone other than the chief executive officer has been strongly opposed in management quarters. The Business Roundtable called the chief executive the link "between the board and the whole operating organization, both line and staff." To snap that link by depriving him of the chairmanship would endanger organizational effectiveness and threaten to create an adversarial relation between the two offices.[18] Nevertheless, it is hard to see how the board can satisfactorily monitor the performance of the individual (along with his staff) who presides over it. At the moment, the tendency seems to lie in the direction of an independent chairman.

Even with a committee structure permitting specialization of tasks, a board whose members served part-time would have trouble simply keeping informed. Such a board would hardly know what questions to ask and would have to rely on data and memoranda supplied by management, how selectively it could not tell. The board's independence under such circumstances would be questionable. This issue was brought to public attention by the resignation of former Supreme Court Justice Arthur Goldberg from the board of Trans World Airlines in October 1972 in a dispute with management over the role of outside directors such as himself. Elaborating on his position in the *New York Times,* Goldberg argued that an outside director "unable to gather enough independent information to act as a watchdog or sometimes even to ask good questions" is presented with an agenda of the board meeting based on decisions already made by management.[19] The kind of "justifiable criticism and legal recriminations" directed against board members that Goldberg linked to this practice came from the SEC in several opinions. In *Stirling Homex* the commission criticized two outside directors: "While they periodically asked general and conclusory questions, they frequently obtained only superficial answers which they accepted without further inquiry." Similarly, in *SEC v. Shiell* the commission noted: "The directors, as outside directors, relied upon the president as their sole source for all information regarding the activities and operations of the company."[20]

Outside directors may, of course, turn to reports by the external auditor, especially in the increasing number of cases wherein outside directors constitute the board's audit committee. I examine this possibility more fully later. For the moment, it is enough to mark that the availability of such independent audits is by itself no guarantee that the board will be informed of matters that may be crucial, nor are such audits—supposedly made in conformity with generally accepted accounting principles—necessarily free from ambiguity or abuse.

Goldberg proposed another solution to the TWA management. He asked that a committee of overseers composed of outside directors be made "generally responsible for supervising company operations on a broad scale," rendering periodic reports to the full board:

> To perform these duties adequately this committee would need authorization to hire a small staff of experts who would be responsible only to the board and would be totally independent of management control. In addition, the committee should also be empowered to engage the services of consultants of the highest competence.

37

As the eyes and ears of the directors, these independent experts and their staff assistants and consultants would look into major policy questions and report to the committee and through them to the board as a whole before decisions are taken on management recommendations.[21]

Goldberg's proposal of a separate committee of overseers found few supporters. Critics feared a split between outside and inside directors and a temptation to overseers to second-guess management, demoralizing the operating staff and destroying organizational efficiency. The further question as to whether the directors, individually or as a board, would benefit from having an independent staff evoked a more divided response.

People who advocate a board composed wholly of outsiders, and a board that would delve deeply into the corporation's affairs—Brown, Stone, and Ralph Nader, among others—have strongly supported the independent staff proposal: "Staff are vital not only in preparing the directors to make informed decisions—gathering information, analyzing management proposals—but also in enabling them, once decisions have been made, to follow up on their directives and ascertain whether they are being adequately carried out."[22] Commentators who eschew a policymaking and emphasize a monitoring role for the board—like Eisenberg, Leech and Mundheim, and the late Neil Jacoby—have tended to oppose a "shadow staff with an institutionalized obligation to second-guess the management, but with very limited responsibility for results."[23] They would rely for accurate and sufficient information on external audits made to the board's specifications. As might be expected, executives of the Business Roundtable have condemned a separate staff for the board as embodying "bureaucratic factionalism."[24]

The question of how much of an independent staff, if any, a board should have, their relation to operating staff, and the nature of their fact-finding function obviously turns on the board's own composition and role. Some corporations provide an independent staffer or two to outside board members, individually or collectively, without formalizing such assistance as an office or authorizing the staff members to engage in any investigative probes. It seems a safe guess that if the board itself becomes more independent of management and institutionalizes its own procedures, a more dynamic staff function will emerge.

How, then, should we assess the responsibilities and liabilities of a board including a majority of independent members? Is *any* change in the construction of their "duty of care," legal or otherwise, needed? This question has several dimensions. Let us first consider the board's responsibility to the corporation's shareholders, which remains, after all, its only generalized obligation other than compliance with laws, usually regulatory, specifically pertaining to the corporation. Two observers, noting the increasing emphasis on a board's committee structure, particularly the monitoring committees (audit, nominating, and compensation), concluded:

> If the standard of care which is demanded of a director is based on an analysis of his functional role within the corporate structure, it is reasonable to suggest that a very high standard might be required of the monitoring directors [on whatever committees they serve]. Precisely because such a director is divorced from traditional management conflict of interest, shareholders may place special confidence in him as the watchdog of shareholder welfare and may rely heavily on the monitoring committee to assure the accuracy of proxy information. This added reliance together with access to internal information may well create a most stringent duty of care. . . .
>
> The modern outside director who serves on an audit committee and has reasonable access to extensive information and sophisticated independent professional assistance and who nevertheless fails to monitor management may well be found to have breached his common law duty of care. . . . Such directors will no longer be able to argue that a gross failure to exercise judgment should be attributed to the management to whom the job has been delegated.[25]

Obviously, this more conscientious performance of a director's monitoring function would take more time than most directors now give. Some corporations have begun to impress upon potential nominees the amount of time expected of them. Texas Instruments now asks a minimum commitment of thirty days a year. In the light of an expanded obligation, possibly carrying significant penalties for nonperformance, the contention that board membership should be made a half-time or even a full-time assignment and compensated accordingly begins to sound more reasonable than at first encounter. If the trend is in the direction of placing enlarged responsibilities on outside directors monitoring a corporation's performance—as seems to be the case—this may very well predicate, if not necessitate, a shift from the more casual part-timer, responsive to management, to the more deeply involved director, exercising an authority to which management is responsive.

This proposal frequently inspires fear that outside directors who take their monitoring duties thus seriously will "try to review operating decisions by substituting their own judgment for that of management" and may be led "to assume an essentially adversary attitude towards management."[26] The Business Roundtable labeled the chief executive officer the "public spokesman" for the enterprise (indeed, for the "larger corporate community" and the "American private enterprise system"), so that any diminution of his position would undermine the effectiveness of the spokesman's role. They advocated "an internal organization which is cohesive, not divided, and which is fast-moving, responsive and flexible rather than bound by excessive bureaucratic regulations or formalities." In this view "political models" are not relevant to an economic organization already subject to government constraints.[27]

Management's concern over a shift in its relations with the board can be understood primarily as reluctance to give up the power it now enjoys over the board. Nevertheless, the clear trend in the contemporary world is toward a sharing of authority and broadened participation in decisionmaking, even at the cost of efficiency. This need not involve the doctrinaire application of political models, as the Business Roundtable feared; presumably, a new relationship between board and operating management requires experimentation. The transition from present to future may not be smooth or swift, but one condition seems clear: the relation between board and management "must be premised on the assumption that both . . . are operating in good faith for the welfare of the corporation.[28] Nothing less is possible if management's tenure is genuinely made subject to the board's determination.

A different problem of adversarial relations is created by the directors themselves through conflicts of interest between the corporation they serve as part-time outside director and another corporation in which they serve as manager (or sometimes, again, as part-time outside director). Chief executives have usually welcomed to their boards people with such affiliations and experience: "Because the corporation is predominantly an economic instrument, a managerial position in another business is a particularly relevant background for service on corporate boards. In our judgment, it is highly desirable for a board to have a central core of experienced business executives."[29] A further consideration, less frequently advanced, is that business executives understand each other and are less likely to make trouble for each other. A certain amount of mutual back scratching encourages board acquiescence in management's actions: the board's monitoring roles can be accepted without being feared. A strictly reciprocal relation—two executives serving on each other's board—is not needed; the collegiality of the corporate world induces a fraternal attitude. Indeed, "virtually all of America's most powerful companies are linked together, directly or indirectly, by the men and women who sit on their boards," as a staff study by the Senate Committee on Intergovernmental Affairs revealed in 1977.[30] Linkages are particularly prevalent between the major financial corporations and manufacturing and commercial concerns. It is noteworthy that no federal agency, including the SEC, maintains any accessible information on the extent of these intercorporate links.

Aside from the fact that directors coming from other companies qualify as outsiders and so are presumed—however unrealistically —to perform their monitoring functions with care and assiduity, there is a further weakness in this practice. The outsider from another corporation is privy to *this* company's inside information; at times he may turn it to his home company's advantage, creating a clear conflict of interests between his roles as director of one company and manager (or director) of another. In effect, he may be in an adversarial relation to the company on whose board he sits; this possibility has been increased by the renewed emphasis on acquisitions, mergers, and conglomerations. This situation was dramatized by the attempt of American Express to take over McGraw-Hill at a time when the former's president was sitting on the latter's board. In a two-page statement in the *New York Times*, the McGraw-Hill chief executive castigated American Express for its "conspiratorial approach" and "unconscionable action." Its president was said to have "violated his fiduciary duties to McGraw-Hill and the stockholders of McGraw-Hill by misappropriating confidential information."[31] While the spotlight momentarily focused on this intercorporate quarrel, reporters noted that the circumstances underlying the conflict were not unusual: "having one foot in each corporate camp in a merger is by no means unique. It may, in fact, be more the rule than the exception in a corporate community where a corporate director commonly serves on the boards of several major companies at one time."[32] And in a revealing introspective mood, the executive of a large company mused to a *Wall Street Journal* staff member: "What can a company really tell its board these days?" His company was then completing a report on internal strategic planning: "We're going over our outside directors one by one and raising questions about potential conflicts. There are plenty. But this report is essential to what we're going to do in the future; *how the hell can we refuse to give it to our board?*"[33] The question this executive's dilemma raised concerning the effectiveness of the board's monitoring role may possibly be answered only when independent board members concentrate their attention on one corporation; again, the trend seems to be toward the more deeply involved director rather than the casual, part-time outsider.

What of the board's relationship to the public at large and to the company's chief constituencies or stakeholders, as they are sometimes called? Brown commented: "Actions expressing the social responsibility of corporations most frequently—although perhaps not always—involve a departure from [the] principle of maximizing the return on investment; and this departure cannot reasonably be expected from executive management, at least to any great extent on a continuing basis." He would therefore place this burden on a board almost entirely of independent directors and especially on its chairman, who would in most instances be a full-time functionary.[34] The Business Roundtable, while placing limited emphasis on "ill-defined social objectives," recognized that long-term profitability requires that corporations "behave ethically and as good citizens." In this self-serving sense, "it is the board's duty to consider the overall impact of the activities of the corporation on (1) the society of which it is a part, and on (2) the interests and views of groups other than those immediately identified with the corporation."[35] Eisenberg would treat the discharge of "relevant nonfinancial objectives," among which he included environmental, consumer, and worker interests, as managerial responsibilities subject to board review through its control over an independent external auditor.[36] Stone, too, argued that "matters of high social concern" should be responsibilities of management, but he would establish statutory or administrative criteria by means of which the board could evaluate management's performance.[37]

Obviously, opinion varies widely over the question of a large corporation's social strategy; I return to this issue shortly, but one last consideration deserves brief comment here. Assigning duties to a board and defining the directors' role provide no guarantee that responsibilities will be satisfactorily discharged. Even making their job a half-time or full-time one or providing some independent staff does not insure that either time or staff will be well employed.

Some pressure on directors to measure up to legal obligations seems necessary. Their present liability to shareholder suits for neglect of duty has been made all but meaningless by judicial construction and directors' insurance. Stone would strengthen a director's sense of obligation both by statutory definition of his duties and by providing a different form of penalty from fines: he would bar offenders from serving as officer, director, or consultant for a corporation for a period of three years.[38] Whether such a deterrent would be regarded as less threatening than an uncertain, court imposed fine or more threatening because it disrupts a career is a matter for speculation. In any event, some motivation for performance—positive and reinforcing or negative and aversive—is needed for directors who monitor no less than for the managers they monitor. I shall reconsider this issue later.

For the moment, let us return to the central thesis of this study: if a new social strategy is needed in order for the large corporation to adjust to and benefit from a changing social environment, then a facilitating alteration of corporate structure is also necessary. From this point of view, the recommendations to reconstitute the board of directors so that it can more effectively appraise corporate (that is, management) performance do not clearly touch the issues. The management performance the board would appraise takes place under existing rules. Stone suggested changing the rules, it is true, to spell out in law "matters of high social concern," core functions that directors ought to be performing, but this is to provide "responsible self-policing" as a substitute for what otherwise might be governmental agency interventions; he expressed primary concern about preventive and remedial measures involving, for the most part, the "wrongs corporations do."[39] Desirable corporate conduct may seek environmental and consumer protection, but this is the sort of thing the Business Roundtable would identify as the ethical behavior of good citizens and Eisenberg would audit as a "relevant" nonfinancial objective within the present framework of corporate interests. When there is concern for social objectives in their own right, as Brown evidenced, no standards exist to guide either board or management. How much social good the corporation can afford remains bounded by its competitive position, its primary legal responsibility to shareholders, and its instincts of good citizenship within those bounds. In fact, what sounds like a considerable corporate restructuring through surgery on the board, either under way or widely deemed necessary, would improve corporate performance only within present guidelines and is unrelated to any corporate strategy involving innovative social programs. The reforms proposed have much to recommend them in their own right;[40] by themselves, they do not move into new territory.

Public Directors

To insure greater responsiveness to interests other than shareholders', recommendations have been made for the nomination of one or more directors by specified groups, most commonly, the employees of a company or their union. The United Automobile Workers demanded such representation in exchange for concessions to Chrysler during the corporation's struggle to avoid bankruptcy in 1979 (the union's president was designated a director in 1980). These proposals need not detain us long. What constituencies besides labor are sufficiently organized to put forward a candidate to represent, say, consumer or environmental interests? There are spokesmen aplenty but few organizations with a broad enough base to support a claim to seat their members on the boards of major corporations.

Although worker directors are increasingly common in western Europe (in the Federal Republic of Germany, which has moved furthest in this direction, half the members of the supervisory boards of corporations with more than two thousand workers are employees or their nominees), labor unions in the United States have shown little interest in going down this avenue of corporate influence. They have preferred to rely on vigorous collective bargaining, which on the whole is more regularized and successful than in Europe. We are thus justified in passing on quickly to a form of board representation that has gained wider interest—public directors.

Growing concern about corporate social responsibility foreshadows organizational change that will give this shadowy concept more definition. At least one aspect of such change concerns the role of the corporate board: "Are directors becoming increasingly responsible to the public at large, rather than to the corporate entity or to the shareholders of any given moment?"[41]

Robert Townsend, the maverick former president of Avis, suggested a decade ago a federal law requiring every corporation with assets of $1 billion or more to support the office of a public director to the tune of $1 million a year for salary (perhaps $50,000 a year) and staff (scientists, accountants, lawyers, and engineers). The manner of the public director's appointment was left open, but one suggestion was selection by a joint committee of Congress whose members would be former business executives. Once approved, directors would be assigned to corporations at random, rotated every four years, and their performance would be reviewed prior to reassignment. The public director or members of his staff would be informed of and could attend "all meetings conducted throughout the company." He "would be required to call at least two press conferences a year and report on the company's progress or lack of progress on issues of interest to the public." Board meetings would be transformed: "Out of sheer shame, other directors would be compelled to help him pursue relevant questions, criticize the answers, and discuss important matters."[42] About the same time Townsend was offering his recommendation, Nader proposed that once a corporation reached a certain size, some proportion—perhaps one-fourth—of its directors should be chosen by popular vote.[43]

The idea of public directors has had a number of other advocates. Stone offered perhaps the most fully articulated proposal.[44] In his version, manufacturing, retailing, and transportation corporations would have 10 percent of their boards filled by public directors for every $1 billion of sales or assets, whichever total figure were higher. In banking, insurance, and utilities the ratio would be 10 percent for ever $3 billion of assets. Stone noted that unless an upper limit were established (say, 50 or 90 percent of the board), the largest corporations would have boards composed entirely of public directors.

Public directors in Stone's formulation would be appointed either by a newly formed Federal Corporations Commission or by the SEC. Appointments would have to be approved by a majority of the corporate board to which the directors were assigned and they could be removed at will by a unanimous vote of the board or for cause by a two-thirds vote. These provisions were intended to offset any suggestion that a public director enjoys greater authority than a regular director. The former does, however, have additional responsibilities and prerequisites: he would spend at least half his time on directorial duties, with an office at the company, and would be paid at the same rate as the highest grade federal civil servant. These public directors would perform a number of significant functions: (1) they would serve as the corporation's superego in the general area of social responsibility; (2) in cooperation with corporate counsel they would oversee the company's compliance with regulatory laws, seeking to obtain internal reform where infractions were found before reporting such problems to the appropriate government agency; (3) they would maintain a liaison with federal and state legislatures and advise on proposed legislation that would affect the corporation; (4) they would check on the effectiveness of the company's internal systems (for quality control, for example); (5) they would provide a hotline to employees—whistle blowers could go directly to them in confidence; (6) they would oversee the preparation of impact statements with respect to new products, processes, and policies; (7) they would provide an interface with the outside world; and (8) they would monitor the effectiveness of board procedures. Like Townsend's public directors, Stone's would have staff and consultants, access to all company records and reports, a seat on all corporate committees relevant to their functions, power to stay the punishment of an employee for cooperating with them, and the right to seek a court order against any internal obstruction of their functioning. Public directors would, however, be subject to the same liabilities for negligence or self-dealing as any other directors.

Despite his goal of reducing government regulation Stone's proposals have drawn a good deal of fire from both management and academicians on the ground that they represent excessive governmental intrusion into the corporation. Critics also have charged that the public director's special status would lead to an adversarial relation with other members of the board, as was said of Goldberg's committee of overseers. The latter criticism might be answered by making all board members of large corporations public directors, so that none would enjoy special status, but this approach leaves open the possibility of an adversarial relation with management.

Suppose for the moment that the logic and spirit of the times are moving toward more involved (perhaps half-time or even full-time) directors of large corporations, whose independence of management is assured by their control of the proxy machinery, the principal committees, and the chairmanship of the board. Would not most, if not all, of Stone's public director functions be considered entirely appropriate to such an independent board? Is it primarily the appointment of public directors by a government agency that smacks of government intrusion, or the working relationship with legislatures and administrative agencies (though most corporations now have at least a semblance of such a relationship)? Possibly some of the opposition to public directors might be removed if their appointment were made not by a typical government commission but by a college of corporate electors composed of representatives of principal private institutions. Would it be possible to create a general sentiment that appointment of public directors by such a group to a major corporation involved a solemn commitment? Service in the public *and* corporate interests, compensated appropriately for the necessary expenditure of time, might prove an attractive opportunity to many qualified individuals, including some now serving as corporate executives (especially those who might be blocked at particular levels from further advancement). Furthermore, if such appointees were given specific obligations (perhaps of the type Stone enumerated), there would be little ground for their failing to comprehend the extent of their duties. Charges of negligence or incompetence might be lodged with the appointive authority and, if such charges were found to be true, the appointment could be terminated or not renewed, rather than a fine levied. To the extent that the office of public director was made an honored position, threatened loss of office for cause might encourage diligence and integrity; penalties for criminal behavior would of course remain applicable.

Would such a board, composed wholly or largely of independent directors, chosen by a public but not a governmental body, be likely to fasten a burdensome internal bureaucracy on the corporation? Presumably the board would be no more bureaucratic than it is now *intended* to be if, in fact, it is adequately performing the overall function of monitoring management's activities. Does this represent the structural change needed if a corporate social strategy is to be made effective? Unfortunately, the answer must be no for the same reason that I gave with respect to the adequacy of a board dominated by outside directors. Simply putting well-intentioned and well-qualified individuals on a board, even if they are called public directors, does not pull a social strategy out of the hat. If the obligations with which they are charged relate largely to protecting the public from misguided corporate behavior or to putting individual corporations on a more dependable course, we still do not have an innovative use of corporations acting in society's interests while taking cognizance of shareholder concerns.

A corporate social strategy must mean that the enterprise undertakes programs specifically in the public interest, going beyond—

without ignoring—production aimed at shareholder benefit. This almost necessitates that the government, society's ultimate representative, provide inducements to nudge the corporation in desired directions—inducements comparable to profits. Yet the inducements should not be so powerful as virtually to compel compliance; they should leave discretionary room in their method of realization, providing genuine opportunity for innovative corporate activity.

What seems necessary is the identification by society itself, through appropriate agencies, of the social objectives it would like to pursue through the large corporations. In the past, this function has been performed largely by the market—a social agency no less than government, though differing in the mode of functioning. The market would continue to perform its role but not exclusively, as in the past. If social functions other than production for consumption are to be performed by the large enterprises, additional, supplementary motivation to this end must tie into the corporation's operations. Precisely for this reason a change in corporate structure is needed. Without such a link, social strategy remains weak and ineffective both for the enterprise and for society at large.

Notes

1. *The Role and Composition of the Board of Directors of the Large Publicly Owned Corporation* (New York: Business Roundtable, 1978), p. 9; hereafter *Roundtable Statement*.
2. Melvin Eisenberg, "Legal Models of Management Structure in the Modern Corporation: Officers, Directors, and Accountants," *California Law Review* 63 (March 1975):376. This and other articles were published in Eisenberg's *Structure of the Corporation* (Boston: Little, Brown, 1976).
3. Myles Mace in a panel discussion, "Functions of Directors under the Existing System," *Business Lawyer* 27 (February 1972):36–37, reporting on his three-year study published as *Directors: Myth and Realty* (Boston: Harvard Business School, 1971).
4. Eisenberg, "Legal Models," p. 391.
5. *Roundtable Statement*, p. 15.
6. Eisenberg, "Legal Models," p. 393.
7. Christopher Stone, *Where the Law Ends* (New York: Harper & Row, 1975), p. 125.
8. Noyes E. Leech and Robert H. Mundheim, "The Outside Director of the Publicly Held Corporation," *Business Lawyer* 31 (July 1976): 1802.
9. Stone, *Where the Law Ends*, p. 139.

10. Courtney C. Brown, *Putting the Corporate Board to Work* (New York: Macmillan, 1976).
11. Eisenberg, "Legal Models," p. 406.
12. *Roundtable Statement*, pp. 19–20.
13. Eisenberg, "Legal Models," p. 409.
14. Leech and Mundheim, "The Outside Director," p. 1827.
15. Brown, *Putting the Corporate Board to Work*, p. 86. Ralph Nader and his colleagues have supplied a variation of this theme: they ask that every director be assigned a particular area of responsibility. R. Nader, M. Green, and J. Seligman, *Taming the Giant Corporation* (New York: Norton, 1976), p. 125.
16. *Roundtable Statement*, p. 20.
17. Leech and Mundheim, "The Outside Director," p. 1830.
18. *Roundtable Statement*, p. 24.
19. Arthur J. Goldberg, "Debate on Outside Directors," *New York Times*, October 29, 1972.
20. Cited by A. A. Sommer, Jr., in "The Impact of the SEC on Corporate Governance," *Law and Contemporary Problems* 41 (Summer 1977): 142.
21. Goldberg, "Debate on Outside Directors."
22. Stone, *Where the Law Ends*, p. 149.
23. Eisenberg, *The Structure of the Corporation*, p. 155. Jacoby's comments took the form of a reply to Goldberg, *New York Times*, December 10, 1972.
24. *Roundtable Statement*, p. 16.
25. Arthur W. Hahn and Carol B. Manzoni, "The Monitoring Committee and Outside Directors' Evolving Duty of Care," *Loyola University Law Journal* 9 (1978): 608, 615.
26. Leech and Mundheim, "The Outside Director," p. 1805.
27. *Roundtable Statement*, pp. 24–25.
28. Leech and Mundheim, "The Outside Director," p. 1827.
29. *Roundtable Statement*, p. 17.
30. Judith Miller, "Interlocking Directorates Flourish," *New York Times*, April 23, 1978, summarizing the Senate committee's findings. David M. Kotz explored the extent and nature of influence of the principal banking institutions in *Bank Control of Large Corporations* (Berkeley: University of California Press, 1978).
31. *New York Times*, January 17, 1979.
32. Karen W. Arenson, "McGraw Rift: Focus on Role of a Director," *New York Times*, January 18, 1979.
33. Priscilla S. Meyer, "McGraw-Hill Puts Outside Directors in Legal Limbo," *Wall Street Journal*, February 2, 1979; emphasis added.
34. Brown, *Putting the Corporate Board to Work*, pp. 20, 42.
35. *Roundtable Statement*, pp. 11–12.
36. Eisenberg, "Legal Models," p. 437.
37. Stone, *Where the Law Ends*, p. 144.
38. Ibid., pp. 147–149.
39. Ibid., pp. 118, 248.

40. Even this view has been questioned. Lewis Solomon of the George Washington University National Law Center examined the results with court appointed independent directors for Mattel, Northrop, and Phillips Petroleum. He concluded: "New directors have been drawn from the same elite as old directors; new boards have not been notably more aggressive than unreformed boards. Moreover, board committees have not given boards much more insight into or control over management activities." Lewis D. Solomon, "Restructuring the Corporate Board of Directors: Fond Hope—Faint Promise?" *Michigan Law Review* 76 (March 1978): 596.
41. Mendes Hershman, "Liabilities and Responsibilities of Corporate Officers and Directors," *Business Lawyer* 33 (November 1977): 285.
42. Robert Townsend, "Let's Install Public Directors," *Business and Society Review* No. 2 (Spring 1972): 69–70.
43. Eileen Shanahan, "Reformer: Urging Business Change," *New York Times*, January 24, 1971.
44. Stone, *Where the Law Ends*, chaps. 15, 16. Stone provided for both general and special public directors; I discuss only the general category.

4

Social Indicators, National Planning, and Corporate Motivation

A mystique has grown up around the idea of the free market. It is sometimes spoken of as though it were a natural phenomenon, subject to disruption only by human interference, or as though it were a religious phenomenon, like the Holy Ghost, to be accepted on faith even if not clearly understood. Of course, the free market is neither of these but a social invention, subject to social control like any other form of planning. The market's "freedom" is a question to be administratively or judicially or legislatively decided; the rules of the free market's functioning have to be determined and enforced.

A considerable body of economic literature has pursued the proposition that large corporations destroy a free market and that to restore the status quo they must be broken up into smaller, competing enterprises; yet large corporations spend millions of dollars every year attempting to keep the public persuaded that so-called private enterprises like themselves are the basic ingredients of a free market. As I noted earlier, the Business Roundtable, composed of chief executives of large corporations, sees as one of the chief executive's functions the defense of this proposition. The free market is thus translated into private enterprise; what is private is free—ipso facto, forget about its inhibiting effects on others.

The theoretical foundation of the free market, laid down and reinforced for a century and a half, lies in the existence of countless homogeneous producers vying for the favor of so many homogeneous consumers that no one possesses any special bargaining power compared with his counterparts. This classic model of free competition is still purveyed in introductory textbooks—along with the numerous reasons, some obvious, some subtle, why the real economy fails to match the model. But since the model has been converted into dogma, examining departures is deemed less important than maintaining the faith. This stance would be unimportant if it were only a philosophical exercise, but as the political rationale for adopting a hands-off policy with respect to the major corporations it has more serious consequences. If, in fact, the large corporations are being pressured into adopting a social strategy, this process is being impeded by the powerful mystique of the free market.

At the root of the issue of society's use of its large corporations for public purposes is the continued questioning of the rights of private property. In the period preceding World War II, the rights of private property had been construed to give management certain prerogatives with respect to employees. Management could make its own rules with respect to the workplace, the tasks to which workers were assigned, the speed at which they were to work, the hours at which a shift began or ended. People unwilling to comply with management-imposed rules were free to go elsewhere—the free market so operated—but the presumption was that the ownership of assets conveyed powers of deciding how those assets were to be used. With New Deal labor legislation and the rapid spread of unionization into mass production industries, the principle emerged that control (ownership or management) over assets did not confer control over workers.

At present we seem to be moving further along the same road, headed toward an ideological destination where the private ownership of property conveys no automatic right to determine to what ends that property will be employed. The private right to own property puts no corollary obligation on society to allow social institutions, constructed out of increments of private property, to be used by property owners at will—even in ways not expressly forbidden.

In the same way that until recently we treated air and water as free goods (hence subject to discretionary private use), we have treated the market as a free good, likewise subject to discretionary private use. But the market, like air and water, is a common good and subject to control in the common good. Social control of the market is not a contradiction in terms, contrary to many interest-oriented pronouncements. The market—where private discretion obtains— operates *within* whatever boundaries society may determine, whether wisely or not. The objective of the boundary lines is to see that "public purposes dominate the orchestration of private energies," as one expositor of the "new political economy" phrased it.[1]

The Not-So-Free Market

In several important respects a free market cannot be equated with private enterprise if by the former we mean a market functioning uninhibited by either private or public controls. The most obvious exception involves private monopoly powers over the production, selling, or buying of goods and services. The late Telford Gaines, a senior official of Manufacturers Hanover Trust, although himself wary of increased governmental intervention, clearly recognized one of the arguments in support of this view.

> In a number of important industries, the recent record shows a pattern of price increases despite underutilization of production capacity. It shows large pay increases for certain organized labor groups despite high unemployment. In economic terminology, these situations suggest that a serious degree of oligopoly control of prices and a monopsony control of wages exist. The notion of the small enterpreneur enterprising in capital intensive industries dominated by giant corporations certainly is not realistic, and the concept of the individual worker bargaining for himself in an organized industry is equally unrealistic. In important respects, our modern economy has outgrown the free market concepts upon which it was built.[2]

Aside from the more straightforward forms of organized exercises of power, there are subtler means of influencing the market: quasibargaining among a small number of corporations; saturation effects of advertising for brand names and generic products; political influence to secure legislation or regulation creating entry barriers in an industry; corporate growth and market domination by the acquisition of potential competitors; and control over innovations by employment contracts asserting claims to any employee's inventions whether or not made on company time or used by the company. Such practices demonstrate that the notion of a free market that no one controls is illusory. Antitrust legislation, though of dubious effectiveness, aims at some of these practices, testifying to the social definition of the market (we shall see that some observers now believe that such legislation no longer defines the market in a way most advantageous to society).

A second disjuncture between private ownership discretion and free use of the market has already been mentioned. Society has attempted to exclude unfair or unethical practices from the market. These constraints have to do less with market control than with market abuse, as illustrated by legislation to insure truth in advertising, truth in packaging, truth in lending, and truth in warranties. Access to the market is contingent on conforming to rules of ethical conduct. In related manner, the market may exclude the products of a company that fails to use its production facilities in ways considered consonant with social interests. Environmental protection laws presumably close the market to firms transgressing standards of pollution control and to products endangering consumer health and safety. Likewise, companies using production processes that jeopardize workers' health and safety are ruled *hors de commerce.* These methods all limit exploitation of the market mechanism to enterprises conforming to certain social standards.

A further narrowing of private discretionary use of the market is now appearing: the establishment of social priorities of production. Private enterprise would be guided to certain categories of production and discouraged, or perhaps barred, from others. Such specification of output, accepted now only in times of national emergency, may become more general in the face of limited resources.

Almost at the time when President Johnson was proclaiming an end to poverty during a commencement address at the University of Michigan, economists at M.I.T., under the sponsorship of the Club of Rome, announced an end to economic growth—not literally an end (though "zero growth" did become a popular phrase) but at least limits to growth that previously had gone unrecognized.

Many quarters have vehemently attacked the limits-of-growth thesis, but it has left behind a disquieting message even among detractors: if growth is possible, its rate is clearly limited; the composition and distribution of a nation's output have become as important as volume. The need to assign priorities in the use of resources has asserted itself. Given that resources are limited, given that incomes are unevenly distributed, and given that some human needs are more pressing than others, it becomes incumbent on society to say that scarce resources should not be used for trivial purposes.

Fletcher Byrom, chief executive officer of Koppers, suggested the change in outlook that may be occurring even on the part of business leaders:

> There may be countering arguments, but I am willing to assume that, in terms of the needs of generations to come, many of the resources we now use and for which we have found no substitutes are in short supply and should be allocated to avoid waste. As a private enterpriser, it amazes me to hear myself say so, but I have serious doubts as to whether we can continue to use price as the sole means of allocation in a time of continuing shortage and inflation. That can only result in placing the greatest burden upon those at the bottom of the economic ladder, who can least afford it. . . .
>
> I, for one, do not believe that Americans can go on eating an average 110 pounds of feed lot–fattened beef every year when we could get 10 to 20 times as much protein out of every acre by eating soybeans and grain products instead of beef. I believe we have to question whether this country can afford to maintain its present pet population and whether we have to produce a moist cat food packaged in aluminum foil, which is a high energy-consuming material. We cannot continue to misuse our resources for life styles that are self indulgent at their best and frivolous at their worst.[3]

The concept of undifferentiated growth (simple increase in GNP) as a national objective, which dominated political and economic thinking for more than two decades following World War II, has been challenged on both moral and physical grounds. Unless we are indifferent to the forms in which assets and income accrue, we must be concerned not only with growth rate but with the composition of assets and income. To treat either GNP growth rate or full employment as independent objectives, without respect to the way national income is consumed or the kinds of jobs in which people are engaged, reflects a materialistic insouciance that many now find shocking. This does not imply a comprehensive ranking of all production along some yardstick of morality or urgency: whatever validity the notion of social priorities enjoys would disintegrate in an attempt to subsume all economic activity under such an ordering. Nevertheless, all production cannot be equally justified amidst present global circumstances. This realization has perhaps been most forcefully underscored by the current international preoccupation with uses and sources of energy: certain forms of energy consumption have been curtailed as less important than others; certain forms of energy production are being encouraged as more promising or less disruptive than others; and distribution considerations—costs of energy to low-income families—have emerged. Andrew Shonfield raised this point in another area:

> If, as seems probable, labor, especially skilled labor, continues to be in short supply in advanced societies by the end of the century, then organizations which are especially well placed to acquire this scarce resource in the market may well be called upon to show, by objective measurement of the performance of labor in their different enterprises, that the marginal product of labor is higher there than it would be if it were employed for some alternative purpose.

"Employment of a social resource like labor requires a social justification," Shonfield argues. "And," he adds, "the intrusion of social costs and benefits into commercial calculations of profit and loss will make for large changes in the kind of enterprise which is deemed to be successful because it yields the highest net rate of return."[4] Such a prospect does not require actual quantification of social costs and benefits for its realization; decisions on priorities can also be made on the basis of qualitative judgments—public policy decisions.

In this context social priorities need not refer only to consumer wants. In western Europe the concept of a national industrial policy has been evolving since the mid-sixties. Although such policy has been hotly disputed, one element is widely accepted: national industrial policy would encourage the development and expansion of industries considered vital to a nation's economic welfare, whether as a producer for domestic needs or as a front runner in international competition. In some instances governments have extended preferential treatment to major corporations considered important in these terms. That in such instances governments are underpinning private enterprises that may be able to hold their own in market terms at some future date does not diminish the fact that social choice has been made outside the market and on behalf of what is considered a social goal. Preference has been expressed by a political decision rather than by a "neutral" market.

A future that would impose greater social limitations and influences on access to the market appears as a further stage in an evolution that began with the *advent* of the market as a system.[5] The market remains—the sphere within which private discretionary decisions are the rule—but market boundaries are constantly being redrafted.

The identification of the free market with private enterprise is being eroded in one further way. In what seems an ever increasing area, development of the necessary instruments of production calls for collaborative effort on a broader than corporate basis. But collaboration among private enterprises, perhaps on an industry basis, requires government participation to give social sanction to the objective so that collaboration does not benefit only private interests; to provide special facilities, financial participation, or the authority of eminent domain; and to relate the undertaking to a wider economic context. Specific proposals for such private-public collaboration have been put forward by the U.S. government with respect to the development of alternative sources of energy and fuel-efficient automobiles. As the research and policy committee of the Committee for Economic Development concluded:

> New hybrid types of public-private corporations may need to be developed to combine the best attributes of government (funds, political capacity, public accountability) and of private enterprise (systems analysis, research and technology, managerial ability) in the optimum mix for dealing effectively with different kinds of major socioeconomic problems such as modernizing transportation, rebuilding the cities, and developing backward regions of the nation. Public-private corporations not only could provide the essential framework for blending government and business capabilities but also could contribute to the synergistic effect that seems to be needed to solve problems that so far have defied conventional attacks.[6]

Foreseeing a reduction in competition vis-à-vis the supply of collective amenities, Shonfield anticipated concomitant social sanctions and influence over such operations:

> An increasing number of services vitally important to the inhabitants of packed and lively urban communities—such services as

57

noise reduction, weather control, or getting rid of air pollution—
will have to be arranged on a collective basis. Once a corporation
has undertaken a contract of this source, it will be difficult for a
community to change quickly to a new supplier if it is dissatisfied
with the results. Again, the corporation will be treated as having
some of the attributes of a public law body.[7]

Clearly, in such an arrangement market principles could scarcely
apply.

Social Guidelines

These varied social restrictions on private access to the market
embody the principle (in Bruce Smith's phraseology) that "public
purposes dominate the orchestration of private energies."[8] What remains to be worked out is the mechanism for achieving this result.
If we lay aside the overdetailed blueprints for a planned economy
that have been crafted by some economists and systems analysts and
think in terms of looser structures, we may be able to discern at
least the direction of change.

At least since Eisenhower's presidency, the country has flirted
with the identification of national goals the nature of which has
remained amorphous. Some commissions have identified philosophical objectives such as greater involvement of people in social
decisionmaking, increased equality, and more opportunities for
self-enrichment in a nonmaterial sense. Others—among them business leaders—sometimes have spoken more specifically in terms of
national income allocations to the most pressing social needs, recognizing that all needs cannot be met simultaneously. One suggestion
that has received support envisions preparation of a social report,
comparable to the president's annual economic report and that of
his Council of Economic Advisers, which "could give social problems more visibility and thus make possible more informed judgments about national priorities." The words come from a document
prepared by the Department of Health, Education, and Welfare,
at the instigation of the president, as a "preliminary step toward the
evolution of a regular system of social reporting."[9] The expected
evolution has not progressed very far, but the underlying idea has
remained alive. In effect, what is sought are social guidelines establishing a framework within which private enterprises can assist in

the realization of specified national objectives while making a profit.

This intention goes considerably beyond the notion that management can legitimize its control of the large corporation by voluntarily assuming a social responsibility, an idea encountered in an earlier chapter. The problem is larger than legitimizing or controlling (regulating) management; advocates of this approach want to give some direction to corporate objectives, in line with social purposes, while allowing discretion in the devising of programs to achieve the wanted results. "In the field of social action, between the minimum duty that compliance with law requires, and the maximum benefit to society that can be achieved within the constraints of the marketplace, there exists a large area for the free play of managerial talent and imagination."[10] Although Bevis Longstreth may be excessively sanguine as to the scope of managerial initiatives "within the [present] constraints of the marketplace," these constraints are by no means fixed: they are subject to social definition. Part of the task is to redraft market constraints in such a way as to induce the desired corporate affirmative actions but within the redefined market.

National Planning

Many observers consider some sort of national planning agency necessary to accomplish this end. Robert Roosa, a partner at Brown Brothers Harriman & Company, expressed concern about the importance of lead time in achieving most major national objectives. He suggested as a modest beginning a three-man council for national planning that would, among its other functions, "appraise possible future needs that have not been recognized in existing government or business programs, and suggest and continually review long-range goals for our American society and economic system." In consultation with other government agencies and public bodies, this council would recommend facilitating legislation. Roosa noted a "compelling need for greater coherence and consistency in the Government's continuing influence in the nation's economic life."[11] Like Roosa, Walt Rostow identified the need for concerted action on major problems before they develop into crises. Like many contemporary economists, he would move away from thinking in terms of Keynesian aggregates and focus on sector needs. He observed

59

that some economists "predict a crisis in the 1980s as severe as the one in the 1930s because of an absolute lack of energy. If we let ourselves wait until that crisis is upon us the lead times, the investment lead times with respect to energy production and conservation, are such that we would have a protracted period of strangulation resulting in tight rationing, chronic unemployment and the like."[12] To avoid such strangulation, forward planning is needed—not just with respect to energy but also in relation to other major national needs. Rostow recommended a central planning unit:

> It is not a question of getting a massive new bureaucracy, but we do need to get a concept of what ought to happen in these sectors. We have got to see the maximum job the private sector can do. We have got to get public policies that allow the private sector to do the maximum and see what the residual costs are for government, meanwhile making sure we have priorities so the balance of the economy isn't excessively distorted.[13]

A theme that runs through both Roosa's and Rostow's proposals is found in many other recommendations: any U.S. system of national planning must be flexible. While such a scheme obviously seeks to direct the efforts of the principal economic institutions to achieve social goals, it must do so with the cooperation of business, relying heavily on the market mechanism. But there is no illusion that the market mechanism is sacrosanct; to the contrary, it is one of society's most valued instruments and its operation can be modified to assist in realizing society's goals, allowing—in Longstreth's words— "a large area for the free play of managerial talents and imagination."

The idea behind planning is to flesh out and refine the concept of social responsibility, now so nebulous and so vulnerable to criticism, by spelling out the relationship between the corporation and the rest of society. This relationship of responsibility may have no more definition than applies to any political person or institution— the president, Congress, a governor, a state legislature—but it needs no less specificity either, so that the discretion accorded the large enterprise is evaluated within the framework of the social purposes for which that discretion is granted.

Such a conception of the political functions of the enterprise seems radical in our day, but it was at least thinkable to a small band of business leaders at the turn of the century, when the organizational revolution was young and the potential of expanded corporate enterprise was breathtaking. George Perkins of the New York Life Insurance Company ventured to a Columbia University commencement audience that the effective control of expanded economic enterprises required experienced managers serving the public, integrated into the federal political structure to give legitimacy to their authority and substance to their responsibility.[14] Charles Steinmetz, the genius of General Electric, was willing to entertain the possibility of corporate managements organizing their operations for public purposes within a system of democratic control.[15]

How the alignment of corporate purpose with national purpose can be achieved while corporations retain a high degree of independence is the political problem that has to be solved. There seems little doubt that an effective solution will require more public-private coordination—"concertation," to use the European term—than has been welcomed in the past. The American tradition has been arms-length bargaining between government and interest groups as the basis for regulatory legislation. In wartime and in the Great Depression public and private representatives did come together to agree on strategies, but these were viewed as short-run, emergency measures. More recently, wage and price advisory policies have come from a tripartite body, but this ad hoc entity has lacked administrative support and connections to broader economic strategy. What seems likely to emerge from the accumulating problems of our times is some mechanism by which the major private economic interests (management and labor in particular) can confer on a continuing basis with government administrators.

It is no simple matter to produce a planning blueprint. Although the object is national policy, there is no identity of interests among the collaborators. Only a bargaining relationship is feasible. With respect to certain wanted actions, the government may have to make concessions to secure private cooperation. In other matters private interests may find it necessary to retreat from preferred positions. The issues are joined not on a piecemeal basis, however, but with respect to the overall result, a result that may stop short of comprehensiveness while trying to locate all the major ingredients of national purpose in the planned relationships. Moreover, national planning would involve more than setting objectives. To be effective, such planning would require a continuing follow-up of results, identification of impediments to the objectives sought, and appraisal of corrective steps. Ongoing monitoring, intended to trigger actions, would necessarily involve concertation, too. With respect to some programs, initiatives could be left wholly to private enterprise, guided by inducements supplementing normal market incentives. In other areas, a greater degree of operational collaboration would be necessary between business and governmental units.

The CED Research and Policy Committee recognized the need for mixed public-service corporations "chartered as needed by appropriate governmental entities: a city, state, group of states in a region, or the federal government."

> The most important characteristic of these public-private corporations would be the best combination or mix of public and private resources to achieve designated objectives.
>
> In general, government's involvement might include:
>
> —A major share of responsibility for financing through appropriations, public borrowing, loan guarantees.
> —*Overall planning so that the corporation's activities fit sensibly into the total environmental system in which it operates.*
> —Public accountability through a board of directors, partially elected and partially appointed, whose tenure (perhaps seven years) overlaps political terms to insulate the corporation from political pressures.
>
> As for business involvement, it might include:
>
> —Managerial and operating responsibilities, harnessing the entrepreneurial drive and managerial skills of the competitive business world.
> —Research and development, in which business has great experience with the kinds of technological systems research and process/product development that are most needed in social improvement.
> —Marketing, in terms of the public-private corporation's distribution of product and services to its customers and their continual adaptation to customer needs and tastes. . . .
>
> The need now is for new, innovative business relationships with government—federal, state and local. Public expectations of more effective social action from both business and government are very great. We believe they call for the renewed appraisal of the respective capabilities and roles of both institutions, and increased creativity in defining relationships between them.[16]

Simon Ramo, former vice-chairman of TRW, offered a somewhat different version of joint planning. Ramo's own and his company's interests explain the special stress he put on the appropriate uses of new technologies:

> To create the new pattern of private-government cooperation, some of us must get over the hangup that insists government is already too involved in the planning of change and should leave the making of advances and the removing of ills wholly to the private sector. Many of the rest of us must abandon the line of thought that says private action is "selfish interest" and bad, so we must become a totally government-directed nation. Almost everyone knows we are actually operating a hybrid society, part free enterprise and part government controlled. . . .
>
> For most of the coming large-scale advances involving resources and technology, effective use of private enterprise resources (even with considerable government participation) will involve private corporations in cooperative efforts that would be precluded by existing, out-of-date, antitrust law interpretations. Our organizational concepts defining the role of business and government were based on an earlier non-technological and non-international society. They must be modified soon to meet the problems of the next 20 years.[17]

Ramo also reflected on the contrast between the right and wrong ways of organizing for the future:

> Doing it wrong . . . means going on without setting goals, without planning, without study of alternatives, with selection by crisis. It means using all of the materials we can lay our hands on, and feverishly building our technological systems, our energy consumption, and our production as though it were our contemplated, determined goal to do so at the highest rate. If such action and our per capita consumption of materials and energy are emulated to the maximum extent by the remainder of the world, then we shall surely create even greater world instability. We shall inadvertently promote contests of increasing severity amongst nations for acquisition and control of resources. Under such circumstances, it is difficult to see how the world can survive to 1990 in any state except one of increasing waste and pollution, fear of each other, and decreasing moral and ethical values. . . .
>
> Doing it right means to discard inhibitions about accepting government-industry-science teaming and deliberate goal-setting activities. It means serious study of socio-technological-economic interfaces, much planning, and considerable control. We must abandon the idea that to articulate objectives and study alternative plans is to embark on a one-way road to a complete state control of the economy and the life pattern. Instead, it may be that to have freedom where it counts will require planning for freedom.

> Neither a state-controlled life nor a completely free-enterprise one will suffice or satisfy us. Instead, new and developing organizational hybrids of varying kinds, depending on the projects to be performed, need to be accepted as the pattern.[18]

As Ramo suggested, liberal quarters have expressed concern over the possibility that such business-government collaboration, with labor included as counterweight, could give rise to a corporatist state, leading to a controlled economy. The semblance of democratic participation would disguise the fact that government without benefit of legislation (or within the framework of very broad, permissive legislation) would extend its authority throughout the economy: "The corporatist purpose is to have simultaneously the substance of State control and the appearance of democracy."[19]

While there are legitimate grounds for exercising care in setting up national planning machinery, refusal to act for fear of the cooptation of private institutions carries caution to excess. Such participation would require a novel working relationship, even a sharing of authority, between the functional authorities (private and public) and the popularly elected representative government, which—next to the constituency itself—is the highest political authority. No clear guides to such a relationship exist; that does not mean, however, that such a relationship cannot be hammered out. Compared with such a pragmatically devised private-public relation, the planning procedure embodied in the Full Employment and Balanced Growth Act of 1978 (the Humphrey-Hawkins bill) seems a heavy-handed expression of good intentions, offending no one and affecting no one. To conceive of planning as simply the superimposition of aggregate goals, supplied by technical experts, on a myriad of ongoing activities is fantasizing.

The public planning ingredient most likely to be overlooked is neither the global projections nor the neat blueprint encompassing all moving parts, the system design beloved by system experts. Economic global and sector projections are of course important to the intelligent organization of a nation's economic effort. In the final analysis, however, neither system elegance nor internal coherence is crucial to a plan's success as much as political sophistication—a sense of what the times require and how the needs can be met at the highest possible level of agreement among the constituent parts. A ragged plan put together by the responsible representative authorities, both in and outside government, with the major pieces of the puzzle sufficiently in place to define the desired result even if some pieces are missing or overlapping is far better than a computer printout that accounts for all the pieces and answers all the questions (however shaky the assumptions on which they rest) but remains an artificial construct, even a technical masterpiece, but not a social strategy.

The Question of Motivation

This brings us finally to the crucial element that would relate social purpose, as expressed in a national plan, to the social strategy of a private corporation. This missing structural link led us to conclude that modifying the composition and functions of the board of directors would be inadequate to carry off a new corporate strategy. Something must be built into the corporation that motivates it to take the kinds of actions conducing to what have been identified as desirable social objectives. As I noted earlier, the profit motive can still serve to encourage corporate activity within the socially delimited market sphere, but by itself profit is not likely to stimulate the expanded range of corporate actions that are needed if the private corporation is to maintain the central economic role it has enjoyed. There are no easy answers to this problem, at best a few indicators. Let us approach the issue tentatively.

The late Eli Goldston, president of Eastern Gas and Fuel, believed that private corporations had capacities for aiding in the solution of public problems. The trick was to enlist those capacities by appropriate incentives. Accepting the corporation as it exists, he laid stress on the "traditional profit motive of business." But for this purpose the market, within which the traditional motive operates, has to be redefined—enlarged, in fact—by government. "The entrepreneurial thrust, *if encouraged, guided, and controlled by the public agencies of our society*, . . . offers the best hope that the deprived and neglected parts of our society can be swept into the mainstream of the economy."[20] Goldston considered it pointless to deplore the expansion of an alliance between industry and government:

But the tools to guide this kind of an alliance must be perfected so that a maximum of social benefit is achieved. We must develop appropriate and controlled incentives that will enable business to deal with such public problems as low-income housing and education; we must find a way to make certain that what is good for business is good for the country.[21]

Injecting social objectives into the market can be accomplished by government contracting with private corporations to undertake specific programs of the kind that Goldston mentioned. The market can be further enlarged by decentralizing some public services. The central government could collect and redistribute revenues and specify minimum standards to be met in the provision of the social services for which revenues were allocated, but within these standards local governments would be free to exercise discretion. From the point of view of building a market for the private provision of public services, decentralization would mean a proliferation of purchasers of the same type of service, as a large number of local governments would form the demand side of the market in contrast to a single central government. We could presume that with a growing but diffused demand for such services, the number of firms competing would also increase, at least in some areas. Thus, more buyers and sellers would help create a more competitive market, with all its attendant advantages, including variety in the provision of social services in respects that did not threaten overall system objectives.

The range of services for which local governments could contract, in line with prescribed national standards, is probably much greater than we realize, running from various types of education to recreation, youth and health programs to housing, cultural activities, pollution control, and waste disposal. Such reorganization of public markets would encourage business firms to direct their research and development activities to social as well as individual wants and to develop new product lines better meeting public needs. The result would be to harness private initiative and innovation in the service of society. By redefining the market to include a larger public sector of competitive activity, public and private objectives could be reconciled. An increase in the public budget designed to provide more adequate social services would carry no more adverse consequence to private business than a decision by consumers to put more of their income into, say, housing than clothing.

The market can also be reshaped to public advantage by judiciously encouraged private investments or by government programs to develop and supply—perhaps below cost—ingredients in a production process that are beyond private capability for one reason or another: "The government subsidizes the production of uranium by making enrichment, processing, research, and other facilities available to private industry at prices that do not reflect the huge capital outlays."[22] In such instances the government would not itself be the consumer, or the only consumer, but by making possible production that could not otherwise have been undertaken, government would insure a supply of goods and services considered crucial to social welfare, thereby helping to make a market.

Providing the market with a new topography drawn to emphasize social interests, along these or other lines, would not necessitate either a new corporate strategy or a new corporate structure. Presumably, their present profit orientation would lead companies to follow the new contours of the market. But this might well be only a first step in a larger design that *would* involve shifts in corporate motivation, which is to say strategy. The next step would almost of necessity be in the direction of diversifying business motives. While profit would remain a major concern, it would cease to be the overriding objective it is today. Kenneth Mason, president of Quaker Oats, signaled the change in emphasis:

> Corporations that control the use of socially important assets have the responsibility to use those assets in a way that makes social sense. . . . Making a profit is no more the purpose of a corporation than getting enough to eat is the purpose of life. Getting enough to eat is a *requirement* of life; life's purpose, one would hope, is somewhat broader and more challenging. Likewise with business and profit.[23]

Mason was specifically concerned with the quality of television programs directed to children and sponsored by business firms:

> In November, 1977, the four largest advertisers of breakfast cereals in this country were asked to testify before the Federal Trade Commission in Washington on this issue. One of the four companies did not send any of its executives to the hearing. Two of the three major advertisers who did show up spoke for several hours, supported by charts, graphs, and film, but never once in their testimony did they acknowledge the possibility that the way commercial television is used in this country to entertain and advertise to young children could or should be improved.
> I think this attitude on the part of broadcasters and advertisers is plainly and simply irresponsible—because it does not make so-

cial sense. U.S. broadcasters have operating control of one of the most economically and socially important assets—the U.S. broadcast spectrum—in the world today. The TV medium is clearly the most pervasive influence in our society. This is particularly true in the case of children, who, by the time they reach college age, will have spent more time in front of a TV set than they will have spent in school, church, or in conversation with their parents.

Commercial television revenues in the U.S. are in excess of $6 billion annually. The advertising revenues for Saturday morning TV alone are around $100 million a year. With that kind of financial backing, broadcasters should be producing programs the nation can be proud of, not ashamed of. The fact that they are not producing such programs means that they and the nation are getting a very poor return on a very important investment, no matter how many dollars they may be reporting as profit.[24]

In similar vein Goldston, deliberately taking issue with Milton Friedman that a corporation's only responsibility is to its stockholders, cautioned a conference of business executives:

It all boils down to whether large publicly held corporations are social aggregations of talent that can be used by a wise government—paying attention to the fact that corporations must make a profit, but not a maximum profit—to accomplish social good. . . .

The great danger of this harping on maximization is that it lets the cheapest louse in every operation say what's good for the country. . . . You can't let the lowest common denominator in American industry seize upon an antique philosophy and use that to justify resistance to corporate participation in moving forward a country that all of us are going to be living in. And the corporation is going to be living long after the management is gone.[25]

If the matter were left in this unsettled state, we would have to rest the significance of corporate social responsibility in motivating business behavior (beyond what profit considerations alone might dictate) on the idiosyncratic responses of individual businessmen, the same ambiguous status accorded it in Chapter 2. But the addition of a national planning mechanism would make for a major difference, especially if we assume that along with specific economic objectives such a plan would incorporate or be accompanied by social indicators of the type elaborated in the HEW pioneering investigation *Toward a Social Report*, cited earlier. We assume that the market is given a changing definition by government actions in accordance with social priorities built into that plan. We likewise assume that the new market opportunities, while offering a profit, do not necessarily offer as high a profit as can be gained in other market operations, so that some added inducement is needed. We further assume that a sense of social responsibility, which might guide a corporation toward areas specifically identified as socially desirable, cannot be relied on, at least in the near term, but requires time and conditioning to develop. At this stage we might fall back on certain flexible instruments that the government has at its disposal to sensitize private enterprise to the importance *to it* of gearing operations to public-interest considerations. Most of these devices are familiar enough—preferred access to credit, loans at advantageous rates of interest, priority in the calendaring of equity or bond issues—but they have been used in an ad hoc manner, sometimes in response to business rather than social interest. In the new framework they would control commercial and financial traffic to give right of way to activities deemed most important.

It may be objected that the use of such instruments amounts to compulsion. Refusal to take the bait may mean, in effect, going hungry. When access to credit or differential tax rates or favorable interest terms is involved, a firm that is not "induced" may find itself at an impossible competitive disadvantage; if not compelled, it is at least coerced, and there is little comfort in the distinction. Nevertheless, when social priorities are at issue, there are valid grounds for exerting such pressure on private organizations. Moreover, there is a difference between induced action and performance under fiat, which would become evident enough when the plan was in process of being drafted, implemented, or amended. The participation of actors responsible for the wanted results would create a bargaining situation in which it could be plausibly argued that business was making social purpose dependent on the satisfaction of its private interests. The fact is that western society must achieve a high degree of compatibility between public and private objectives in order for any form of planning to be effective.

Another device that has become important not only in the United States but also in western Europe is the conditional contract. The U.S. government annually contracts for goods and services valued at billions of dollars. By requiring that the recipient of a contract (at least above some dollar amount) conform to certain standards (nondiscriminatory employment policy, for example) the government is in a position to penalize noncomplying companies. This approach was tentatively used beginning in 1978 to deny federal contracts exceeding $5 million to firms not conforming to wage-price guidelines. The order was challenged in the courts as an unauthorized system of mandatory controls, with the government contending that, on the contrary, compliance was optional even though access to contracts might be an important consideration to a company. The battle followed a shifting course through the federal judiciary, a district court finding that the threat of ineligibility would be for some companies the most severe possible sanction the government could impose and hence an unwarranted exercise of executive power; a circuit court found legislative sanction in a 1949 act authorizing the government to procure supplies in a manner "advantageous to the Government in terms of economy and efficiency"; and the Supreme Court upheld the latter ruling by refusing to review the case.[26]

The government's influence as contractor could also be used more affirmatively by awarding contracts to firms demonstrating initiative and zeal in socially beneficial, nonmarket areas, emphasizing but not necessarily limited to objectives specifically identified in a social report. (Contractual preference might be given, for example, to a firm showing greater concern for the psychological and educational impact of its television programs, in line with Mason's strictures.) Thus, a government contract could reward the enlightened use of corporate assets in society's interests. A firm might be motivated to excel in some particular way that distinguished it from others competing for contracts. In contrast, denial of a contract to punish noncompliance with regulatory standards would motivate a firm only to a minimum performance consistent with qualifying as a government supplier.

The motivation would be reinforced if, as Goldston believed, "strong forces are pushing business to face the major problems of our society"[27] and, as Longstreth noted, there is a trend among institutional investors "to concern themselves with the social aspects of corporations in which they have invested."[28] Unfocused, such forces and trends are likely to be ineffective, but they could become significant if coupled to broadly identified social indicators and the positive reward of profitable government contracts. Constructive corporate programs in line with defined social priorities would mark a move toward a reorientation of corporate strategy. The 3M Company has taken a step in this direction in its pollution prevention program, the goal of which is to shift the thinking of company managers from pollution cleanup to the redesign of products and processes to prevent pollution from occurring. The company's chief executive commented that since the government was unlikely to let up on pollution control, it made sense for the company's employees to think more positively about eliminating the problem itself. As a government official added: "The next stage will be to design pollution control in from the start."[29] Here again, corporate programs that are not limited to regulatory compliance but advance to affirmative actions along lines that have been demarked by public policy can be reinforced by governmental recognition through contract awards.

Shonfield carried the matter of corporate motivation into open territory with the assertion that few people believe that corporate managers should concern themselves primarily with maximizing the welfare of a shifting group of shareholders. This challenges—as he recognized—the "whole notion of ownership in relation to corporate enterprise." We are back where we started, returning to the root issue of the rights of private property. The present legal short-term interests of the owners of large corporations cannot be made the guide to corporate policies that affect the long-run interests of society at large: "Different interest groups" crowd in on the company and demand a right to be heard; "the state itself may be expected to wish to assert its right to influence the management decisions of giant corporations."[30]

These largely inchoate present efforts to affect corporate actions can reasonably be expected to take on clearer institutional form as pressures mount for more effective social use of the large corporation. Concerted national economic planning would seem to be nearly inescapable, along with a clearer definition of related non-market social priorities inviting corporate initiatives, and it would be surprising if there were not rewards for such socially oriented activity in the form both of public recognition, which would be psychologically rewarding, and of public contracts or preferential treatment, which would be economically rewarding.

Economically rewarding to whom remains a thorny question if shareholders' claims are to be scaled down—rewarding perhaps to the corporation's employees for their ingenuity and effort in devising and carrying through the programs that are rewarded or perhaps to the corporation as an entity, to provide it financial capability in further pursuing its more socially conceived endeavors. In any event, motivation will change with the adoption of a new corporate strategy based on the discretionary exercise of the powers that inhere in the large-scale organization, a discretionary exercise of power that would now be oriented toward broader social interests. The question of whether individuals and institutions would continue to invest in corporations if their prospective earnings were reduced may be answered in several ways. An assured rate of return would, as with bonds, prove attractive to some. Investors might be given a share in capital appreciation or enjoy an increase in the earnings rate if their company placed itself among the best social performers. The primary consideration would be whether there were preferable alternative forms of investment, a matter that would involve, as now, a social definition of the capital markets. In any case, a share in profit by the corporate entity would, again as now, facilitate self-financing, and preferential government treatment would further assist the corporation to pursue a social strategy.

If institutional changes along these or related lines should occur, resulting in a revised corporate strategy, the need for an accommodating structure would become evident. At this point the rationale for a corporate board composed of public directors would be clearer. Such a board would appoint and monitor the chief executive and his cabinet but in line with a broad public agenda of economic and social priorities. This development would not eliminate government regulation of corporate behavior, to be sure, but should diminish the need for such intervention.

The type of hybrid organization—part public, part private— that the CED and Ramo envisaged is also likely to become important in the foreseeable future. But, again, to the extent that large corporations can be motivated to respond more readily to social demands, their own expanded initiatives may reduce the need to rely on hybrids.

Notes

1. Bruce L. R. Smith (ed.), *The New Political Economy: The Public Use of the Private Sector* (New York: Wiley, 1975), p. 14.
2. Telford Gaines, "The U.S. Economic Tradition," *Economic Report* (New York: Manufacturers Hanover Trust, January 1976), p. 4.
3. Fletcher Byrom, "Corporate Policy Applied to a Finite World" (address, Woodlands, Texas, October 21, 1975), pp. 7, 15.
4. Andrew Shonfield, "Business in the Twenty-first Century," *Daedalus*, Winter 1969, pp. 205–206.
5. Karl Polanyi, *The Great Transformation* (New York: Holt, 1944).

6. Committee for Economic Development, *Social Responsibilities of Business Corporations* (New York: CED, 1971), p. 59.
7. Shonfield, "Business in the Twenty-first Century," p. 200.
8. Smith, *The New Political Economy*, p. 14.
9. U.S. Department of Health, Education, and Welfare, *Toward a Social Report* (Washington, D.C.: GPO, 1969), pp. xii, iii.
10. Bevis Longstreth in a panel discussion, "Corporate Responsibility Panel: The Role of the SEC," *Business Lawyer* (March 1973): 227.
11. Robert V. Roosa, "Economic Planning: A Middle Way," *New York Times*, February 8, 1976.
12. Walt W. Rostow, "It Will Take Skill to Avoid a Boom," *New York Times*, May 21, 1978.
13. Ibid.
14. George W. Perkins, "The Modern Corporation" (New York, 1908), reprinted in Moses Rischin, *The American Gospel of Success* (Chicago: Quadrangle, 1965), pp. 109–118.
15. James B. Gilbert, "Collectivism and Charles Steinmetz," *Business History Review* 48 (Winter 1974): 520–540.
16. CED, *Social Responsibilities of Business Corporations*, pp. 60–61; emphasis added.
17. Simon Ramo, "Technology and Resources for Business," in X. Smith (ed.), *A Look at Business in 1990*, summary of the White House Conference on the Industrial World Ahead (Washington, D.C.: GPO, 1972), pp. 146–148.
18. Ibid.
19. J. T. Winkler, "Law, State, and Economy: The Industry Act 1975 in Context," *British Journal of Law and Society* 2 (Winter 1975): 125.
20. Eli Goldston, "New Prospects for American Business,' *Daedalus*, Winter 1969, pp. 78–79; emphasis added.
21. Ibid., p. 79.
22. Richard J. Barnet, "The World Resources," *New Yorker*, March 17, 1980, p. 71.
23. Kenneth Mason, "Responsibility for What's on the Tube," *Business Week*, August 13, 1979, p. 14.
24. Ibid.
25. "The 'Responsible' Corporation: Benefactor or Monopolist?" *Fortune*, November 1973, p. 56.
26. *New York Times*, June 1 and 23, 1979; *Wall Street Journal*, September 3, 1979.
27. Goldston, "New Prospects for American Business," p. 86.
28. Longstreth, "Corporate Responsibility Panel," p. 235.
29. "3M Gains by Averting Pollution," *Business Week*, November 22, 1976, p. 72.
30. Shonfield, "Business in the Twenty-first Century," p. 201.

5

The Corporate Social Audit

Within recent years a number of companies have experimented with social audits—a term rejected by some as misleading but catchy enough to have stuck. One of the early exponents, the late Raymond Bauer of the Harvard Graduate School of Business Administration, once commented that "in the fall of 1971 I knew of about a half dozen companies that were trying it. By the beginning of 1972 the number had jumped to a dozen. Now [fall 1973] . . . virtually every large company I know of is trying or thinking of trying a social audit or something like it."[1]

The nebulous nature of the new device was all too evident. As Bauer reported, typically the idea would come "from somebody at the very top, and subordinates [did] not know exactly what was on his mind, nor [did] they have access to him to check whether or not the subordinate and he [were] thinking alike, or could learn to think alike. . . . some of the most important executives are doubtful about the whole idea."[2] With the passage of time, some of the ambiguity but little of the ambivalence surrounding the corporate social audit disappeared; increasingly popular, this technique is now generally understood to refer to a compilation of information about the social impact of a company's activities and its objectives in certain social areas, along with a report on how well the firm is

74

doing with respect to these objectives. (The American Institute of Certified Public Accountants carefully distinguishes between a social audit, which includes social objectives, and social information, which is an input to the process of deciding on objectives and assessing results,[3] but the distinction is difficult to maintain.) The method of reporting varies considerably: a few paragraphs or pages in the annual report are the most common form, but certain companies issue supplementary statements of varying length on an annual or irregular basis. Most social audits include only favorable information; a limited number provide balanced statements.[4]

What Purpose Social Reporting?

If there is now more agreement on the general characteristics of a corporate social audit, there is still considerable divergence of opinion on the specifics. Even so fundamental a matter as its purpose is subject to dispute. Basically there are two camps—those who believe that the corporate social audit is a management tool, for internal use, and those who believe it is, in addition, a system of disclosure that a company owes to the public.

In 1974 the Committee for Economic Development sponsored a survey of business social reporting and assessment. Of 750 companies to which questionnaires were sent, 284—mostly large corporations—submitted usable replies:

> When asked what purpose or purposes led management to undertake a social audit, a small minority attributed their action to the felt need for public disclosure or to their desire to "meet public demands for corporate accountability." When asked to whom the results of their audits were disclosed, the response indicated that less than half these companies made their findings available to their stockholders and the public.[5]

Fifty-three percent confined the results to executives or directors. Obviously, most companies viewed such reports as internal documents.

This position was made transparently clear in supplementary comments:

> Some of the explanations of purposes were: "as a guide to internal management," "part of marketing strategy," "part of long-range

75

planning," "to broaden experience and thinking of managers," "to extend markets with minorities and government," "to determine priority and urgency," "to balance commitment to social activity against job activity," "to help those who need jobs and housing," "to provide source material for executive speeches and public statements," "to develop some reward-accountability for managers," "to make sure the company is fulfilling its promises and commitments," and "to provide comprehensive response to many inquiries in this area." An examination of these statements reveals that most corporations that have undertaken the inventorying and assessing of their performance in the area of social activities have done so for corporation-centered reasons.[6]

Some corporations (Atlantic Richfield, BankAmerica, International Paper, among others) use social audits to set guidelines for managerial actions, at times basing financial compensation in part on the realization of assigned and budgeted objectives of a social nature (perhaps a proportion of minorities or women hired). In more general terms, the audit is considered "part of the strategic and operational planning process" with respect to identified social objectives.[7] This corporation-centered attitude was acknowledged by the Task Force on Corporate Social Performance of the U.S. Department of Commerce when in 1978 it sought to allay business suspicions after proposing an "index of social performance." Originally, this was to measure corporate responsiveness in such areas as minority hiring, environmental controls, and attentiveness to consumer interests, but an outcry from major business associations served to shift its intended purpose. The index would constitute a

> guide . . . available to interested companies to use internally to help measure and manage the impact of their operations on the community. It would permit a corporation to determine the kinds of activities it wished to pursue, set its own goals, evaluate its progress through self-measurement, and improve program management. A "review" would be descriptive, not prescriptive, and its use would be entirely voluntary.[8]

Later the proposal was dropped altogether.

Even observers who regard a corporate social audit in this light are usually not averse to publishing those portions that are likely to improve the corporate image. The more serious question is whether, once a company adopts the practice, the public is *entitled* to see the results. David Linowes, a leading advocate of social auditing, strongly urged this position. He sees a "social audit and reporting system" as a "monitoring and measurement network" providing a "dispassionate evaluation" of a corporation's contribution to social welfare. "The public is entitled to no less."[9] Eschewing quite so dogmatic a position, the American Institute of Certified Public Accountants (AICPA) nevertheless agreed that whatever form it takes, the corporate social audit should "establish and communicate the social impacts of business actions on those who are affected by them."[10] About half the corporate respondents of the CED sponsored survey, most of whom construed a corporation's social report as basically a tool for internal use, conceded that such reports would probably be required in the future, an outlook that could hardly be premised on any expectation but their availability to the public.

It seems evident that business thinking on the internal versus external use of corporate social reports depends very heavily on the nature of the report. If the document is something of the company's own devising, neither mandated nor prescribed in form, most companies are prepared to release their tailored statements to the public, perhaps even engaging in a little self-criticism to give the report credibility (as Eastern Gas & Fuel admitted: "Our industrial accident record in recent years has not been good.")[11] But compulsory disclosure in specific areas meets strong resistance: "The buffeting which business has taken at the hands of the public during the last decade has made executives wary about divulging sensitive and complex information."[12]

Comprehensive versus Selective Reporting

As the AICPA noted, an ideal system of social reporting would produce information about "each and every cause-effect relation" arising out of the impact of business operations "on the quality of life of all significant segments of society."[13] The result would be a kind of operating statement and balance sheet of a company's social effects, whether the effects were intended or not. The rationale behind such comprehensive reporting is to "net out" the beneficial and the adverse. Linowes provided an example: "A nationally known mining and manufacturing company annually ravages and defaces untold acreage in a dozen U.S. states, converting virgin stretches of land into unsightly eyesores via strip mining procedures. . . . The same company contributes thousands each year to community renewal and neighborhood improvement programs."[14] Even for purposes of guiding management policy, concentration on one of these aspects to the exclusion of the other would be poor practice. From the public point of view this approach would be crudely misleading. In some instances companies may even intend to mislead. Indeed, "a study by the nonprofit Council on Economic Priorities makes the situation clear: 'Those companies which tend to contribute most to pollution also tend to toot their horns most blaringly about the contributions they make to pollution control.' "[15]

Despite the danger that selective reporting of a corporation's social impact can be abused, there is little way to avoid selective reporting. The CED put the matter in perspective:

> As yet there are few indications as to how corporate executives, other than by seat-of-the-pants judgments, can determine which expectations deserve priority among those being communicated to [them] by reformers, consumer advocates, some shareholders, the practices of other corporations, and government. Much of what is communicated through these channels (other than the actual enactment of legislation) is distorted by emotions, or is infeasible. The corporate executive, hence, is left with the necessity of weighing the messages conveyed via the channels other than legislation and deciding what expectations have gained such general acceptance among consumers, employees, stockholders, and citizens as strongly to suggest, if not require, his taking action. The corporate executive's problem is one of determining what social problems are of such critical and continuing consequence to the constituencies his firm serves as to warrant the company's acceptance of some measure of responsibility for aiding and for shouldering the associated costs and obligations.[16]

The AICPA, while recognizing the desirability of comprehensiveness, retreated to a "social information system capable of implementation within a decade," which means that "not all social phenomena will be measured; instead, emphasis will be given to significant actions and impacts affecting areas of primary social concern."[17]

Selective concern has almost of necessity been the path followed by companies that have experimented with social audits. While the selection process sometimes has been influenced by the potential for public relations puffery, other criteria have been the presumed relative degrees of public interest, the possibility for effective organizational implementation of a given program, and a company's special capability in particular areas.

The first report of Eastern Gas & Fuel, *Toward Social Accounting*, published in 1973, concentrated on four social performance categories:

> The topics for this report were not chosen because they are necessarily the most important ones, or the ones that might make us look good, but because they are the most readily measurable, because our goals with respect to them are comparatively simple and clear, and because they lie in areas where management can rather directly influence results. In addition, managerial decisions on those topics can have a significant impact on earnings per share.[18]

The life and health insurance industries have jointly established a Clearinghouse on Corporate Social Responsibility, to which some two hundred member companies report: "This Social Reporting Program has two primary objectives: (1) to provide an industry profile by which individual companies can compare their own programs, and (2) to demonstrate to the public the degree of accountability and commitment of insurance companies in this vital area."[19] However,

> a social performance program can't cover the waterfront. The Clearinghouse in 1972 sought the inclusion of only those activities which linked the predominant resources of the business with the priority needs of the community and of the larger society. So, we came forward with six: Community projects, contributions, equal employment practices, social investments, voluntarism and environment (later adding to this, energy conservation).[20]

The Matter of Measurement

Along with the question of the scope of a corporate social audit goes the question of methodology or form. The principal issue here has been whether—in line with the concept of an audit—emphasis should be placed on quantitative reporting or, since not all social issues readily lend themselves to quantification, whether descriptive statements, along with a variety of measures, are acceptable.

Advocates of quantitative measurement argue that this approach is subject to verification and will tend to reduce self-serving rhetoric. Moreover, quantitative reports permit comparisons of social performance among companies and facilitate calculation of the costs incurred to obtain the social objectives sought. For those who believe in a comprehensive audit, with a net balance of social costs and benefits, quantitative measurement yields a summary figure of a company's social contribution, a bottom line.

To obtain this last presumed advantage, it would be necessary to have a common unit of measurement for all the types of programs being assessed: "In such a system, specific actions and impacts would be measured in terms of the characteristics of the specific matter being measured. Subsequently, they would be converted to a common unit" that could be compared, added, or subtracted.[21] The AICPA even proposed the creation of a special unit, a "social measurement utile" (SMU), treading on ground that Jeremy Bentham worked over almost two centuries ago, when he sought to develop his "felicific calculus" for purposes of determining what actions conduced to the greatest good of the greatest number. But, also like Bentham, the AICPA seems to lean toward the view that *if* a common denominator is to be found, it will be a pecuniary one.

Champions of balance sheet accounting clearly prefer the dollar measure. For one thing, dollars are the language of business. Linowes conceded that pecuniary measurements of social actions may initially be imprecise, but he argued that techniques can be improved with experience. Moreover, "the softness of much of the economic and fiscal data used today, as well as the frequency with which it is misused, leads one to suspect that given all their present limitations, social measurements may be just as reliable." Linowes advanced several rules that would help identify the items to include in a "socioeconomic operating statement" (SEOS). For example, "if a socially beneficial action is required by enforceable law and regulations, it is not included on a SEOS statement." He also listed specific items that would appear on an SEOS as positive action—the cost of a voluntarily established nursery school for children of employees and the salary of an executive while serving on a government committee. A negative social action might be the cost of a safety device recommended by the Safety Council but not installed.[22]

In 1973 Clark Abt came forward with the most comprehensive and complex social audit theretofore devised, based on a social income statement and social balance sheet, "which included calculations of every conceivable cost and benefit of a company's social impact, often through the use of 'shadow prices.' "[23] Although Abt's effort excited a good deal of interest and comment, the response was overwhelmingly negative. Daniel Gray, consultant to Arthur D. Little Co., called it a "long, elegantly appointed blind alley":

> The notion of recording all relevant human and social phenomena into dollar amounts in the way Linowes and Abt are trying to do . . . seems to us basically unsound. . . . The reason why it seems basically unsound to us to try to apply traditional business accounting to these "externalities" is that prevailing accounting is married to and therefore bounded by the same limits as the prevailing theory of a market economy. Like that theory it focuses on the world of transactions. But the very problems we want this accounting to cover have become problems precisely because they lie outside the world of transactions. Profit and loss accounts derive directly from a theory that could only achieve closure by expressly excluding what it calls "external diseconomies" and we call "unrequited social demands." It will take not an act of stretching but an act of invention to produce a calculus that will encompass those demands.[24]

Bauer likewise found flaws, both philosophical and conceptual, in the balance sheet approach. Can we, he asked, like Gray, express social benefits and liabilities in dollar terms, with any credibility, precisely at a time when there is widespread questioning of the *social* significance of market values—of what, for example, GNP means in terms of social values?[25] What of the fact that "often a company can make its most important social contribution by adopting policies for which there is no identifiable cost, but which may be socially very positive, such as enlightened marketing and advertising practice"? Similarly, a more competent management, which through good engineering had designed in pollution control procedures, would be found—under a dollar measurement system—to have made less of a social contribution than a company with poorer technical capabilities that had had to invest in pollution control equipment to compensate for its less efficient technology.[26]

The difficulties inherent in a balance sheet approach to social auditing have led most experts to embrace a less systematic but still serviceable form. Arthur Toan, Jr., who chaired the AICPA's Committee on Social Measurement, advocated a corporate social profile that, while incomplete and lacking a common unit of measure, would "describe the company's actions and impacts in selected important areas, using whatever units of measurement, qualitative description and bases of comparison that most fairly and informatively characterize corporate activity."[27] The AICPA report—not surprisingly reflecting Toan's position—identified an initial system, achievable in the near term, in which "measurements will be made of selected attributes chosen because they indicate the essence of actions taken and impacts made by the company. A variety of units of measure will be employed, and narrative descriptions will be used where quantitative measurements are not practical."[28]

To the CED researchers, mulling over the variety of views expressed by their corporate respondents, "one thing, however, seems clear. The social audit will evolve as a means of meeting society's demands for a fuller accountability. In time, although not necessarily soon, a consensus as to its content and form acceptable to both corporations and their constituents will develop."[29] These analysts found the present stage of diversity a necessary preliminary to an ultimate conventional form of corporate social reporting, the development of which is virtually assured by pressures building to that end.

The Problem of Credibility

A final question pertains to the agency undertaking the corporate social audit. Should the corporation review and appraise its own operations or should that function be performed by an outside agency, comparable to the external (public) auditor? Given the present state of corporate social reporting—wholly voluntary, necessarily selective—and given widespread corporate qualms about possible adversarial use of any reports including critical commentary, virtually all companies have insisted on retaining firm internal control over what information is released to the public. The result has been blandness, even smugness, in what purports to be objective reporting.

A few companies have attempted to meet this problem. While retaining internal control over report preparation, they have sought to minimize the self-congratulatory tone and emphasize content. BankAmerica is an outstanding example. A task force consisting of seven senior executives, extensively consulting with department heads, initially prepared a "voluntary disclosure code" identifying "general categories of information" of interest to the bank's several constituencies and the public at large. Guidelines were provided to assist operating personnel in applying the code, and a separate office was created to supervise and disclose the details of the corporation's social policies and actions, which are summarized in an annual publication entitled *Community and the Bank*. The reporting system is linked to the actual conduct of the company's social programs by institutional arrangements, heading up to two principal committees:

> One committee is the Public Policy Committee of the bank's Board of Directors. It includes a dominant majority of outside directors, and meets monthly. The committee's functions include identification and monitoring of broad environmental, political and social trends that could affect the bank's activities or performance, and advising management on long-range plans and programs to keep bank activities in consonance with emerging social requirements. In addition, the committee reports to the full board on the status and adequacy of the bank's overall policy activities and presents specific recommendations for improvement, as necessary. . . .
> The Social Policy Committee brings together senior managers from many operating and staff departments. It is chaired by a senior officer who heads the bank's Social Policy Department, the staff arm of the committee and a support group for the directors' committee as well. . . . It is charged with setting priorities and standards for responsible action and initiating changes in bank policies, positions, and practices.

The individuals involved in bank operations are identified in the company's public report, thus "reinforcing the bank's pledge to maintain an open door to employees and all outside parties interested in obtaining additional information about specific activities or providing their own input to the formulation of policy in specific areas." BankAmerica emphasizes the voluntary nature of its commitment to consistent and systematic disclosure of its social policies and programs: "How it makes that disclosure, providing it does so in conformity to self-imposed disclosure standards, is entirely within management's discretion."

> The point here is that, unlike a mandated social audit or a regulatory scheme, the company can experiment with form and organization, as well as subject matter and detail, to fashion a document, or series of documents, best suited to fairly and fully inform those of its constituencies who say they need this information to judge the company's performance.[30]

Most corporations have not attempted this kind of effort to gain credibility for internally generated social reporting, but problems of credibility remain even with BankAmerica's exceptional performance. The AICPA identified a number: what is to be measured or reported cannot be completely defined and in any event is selective, so that "their appropriateness will not automatically be accepted. . . . Since the information produced will be incomplete in coverage and will have a broader than usual range of accuracy, its 'vagueness' will be a source of questions. When norms or standards of comparison are employed, particularly those implying amounts or degrees of responsibility, the extent of their acceptance by groups holding different views about corporate roles will vary. . . . Since the report will be that of management, its objectivity will have to be established with those who may suspect it to have self-serving purposes."[31]

When General Motors' annual *Public Interest Report* relates the corporation's costly efforts to comply with the Clean Air Act, readers are likely to put the company's commentary into their own context of remembered corporate and industry resistance to such regulations. The social audit may then appear less than complete, perhaps even misleading. Atlantic Richfield tried to gain credibility for its admittedly upbeat social report, *Participation*, by the unusual device of appending an unedited critique written by a syndicated columnist known to be critical of irresponsible business behavior. The 1977 critique, running to six pages, included a three-page balance sheet of the company's social assets and liabilities.[32]

The CED sponsored report recommended two courses of action to win public acceptance for a company's self-appraisal:

> The first step is the retention of an independent analyst to examine the corporation's performance and to prepare and certify the report. Qualified independent analysts are scarce, but a few of the national management consulting firms, a few of the national accounting firms, and a few members of the faculties of graduate schools of business possess the requisite competence.
>
> The second step is to have a committee composed of the members of the board of directors (including public directors) review and approve the social report. . . . The committee's review and approval of the independent report would be essentially analogous to the action of the corporate audit committee, which in many corporations meets with the independent accountants, reviews a draft of their financial report, and approves this report before it is promulgated to the stockholders and to the public.[33]

Linowes basically agreed with CED's recommendations. Although socioeconomic operating statements "would be prepared internally, they should be audited by an independent interdisciplinary team, headed by a CPA."[34]

The analogy between the social audit and the financial audit and the consequent image of a CPA as capable of providing an objective external check on social reporting by internal management have created discomfort in the accounting profession. Many leading accountants have expressed unwillingness to be drawn into so murky and undefined an area, fearing that their carefully guarded reputation in their traditional field may be tarnished by inevitable stumbling in the new territory. The AICPA Committee on Social Measurement was less hesitant:

> If the profession wishes to adopt a posture of not auditing any social information until *all* can be audited, or of leaving such auditing to a new profession, it can, of course, do so, assuming society will permit it. However, the option that seems preferable is for the profession to attempt to move along with improvements in social information and, in fact, to influence the course of development of social measurement in a way that will reflect the auditor's needs.[35]

The auditor, the committee added, may find it necessary, or at least helpful, to call on the services of nonaccounting experts in forming his opinion.

Voluntary or Compulsory Reporting?

"Despite the growth, over a decade or more, of public opinion that corporations should do more for the social good, the American corporation does not yet have an established obligation to render an accounting to anyone on its overall social performance."[36] This observation by John Corson and George Steiner, who undertook the investigation on social reporting sponsored by the CED, can be complemented, as we have seen, by the observation that the overwhelming majority of American corporations resist such an obligation. Nevertheless, almost half the firms responding to the CED questionnaire (and almost three-fifths of the largest corporations) expected that a social audit would be required of them in the future.

In recent years the SEC has been subjected to pressure, chiefly from environmental groups, to require public disclosure of corporate actions affected by the major antipollution laws. In 1971 the SEC complied with guidelines, revised in 1976, requiring that corporations disclose:

> (1) the material effects that compliance with federal, state and local environmental protection laws may have upon capital expenditures, earnings and competitive position of registrants, (2) all litigation commenced or known to be contemplated against registrants by a government authority pursuant to federal, state or local environmental regulatory provisions, and (3) all other environmental information of which the average, prudent investor ought reasonably to be informed.[37]

Pressures on the SEC to force further corporate disclosures in areas of social interest have not abated. The agency has been urged "to give serious consideration to the formulation of guidelines aimed toward expanding the scope of information concerning the social impact of corporate activities."[38]

This approach through securities legislation rests the requirement for such disclosures on whether the latter are material *to an investor*. But the investor's interest may in due time become the vehicle for more general public interest. As Longstreth observed: "It would appear that many investors today consider a broad range of social aspects of business activity to be 'material,' in the sense that such matters, if known, may affect the investor's desire to buy, sell, or hold a company's securities."[39] But the SEC is reluctant to extend its authority so broadly by administrative construction. A generous interpretation of materiality, as SEC Commissioner Phillip Loomis commented, would give that body a "roving commission to require American industry to do anything we think would be a good thing for them to do." Traditionally, the SEC has held that materiality to an investor involves a "dollar and cents impact." To depart from that tradition would require a determination that materiality can relate to matters having no bearing on a company's financial position. "And," Loomis concluded, "the verdict is not in on that, in my submission."[40]

Once again we seem to be up against a movement to redefine the rights of property. Loomis was undoubtedly correct in asserting that the SEC, charged with safeguarding property interests, is the wrong place to lodge broader social concerns. But in that case, and if the forces urging a social role on the large corporation are real and continuing, then this may amount to saying that the role of the SEC in monitoring the corporation, like the constituent interest of the shareholder-owner, is in fact diminishing and that some new agency—or perhaps modified institutional relationships—may have to be put in place to satisfy the evolving need. "What it boils down to," Linowes observed, "is that we cannot reasonably or realistically expect to achieve nationwide corporate social responsibility on a voluntary invisible basis. Inevitably, when volunteers are called for, a handful respond, the majority remain mum."[41]

The future of the corporate social audit is certainly not clear. What is clear, however, is that there is a significant—if somewhat ambivalent—interest in the concept among a relatively small number of corporate leaders; a much larger number is trying to work out a variation of the idea that will benefit them internally and help set themselves straight with an amorphous public; a surprisingly high percentage of major corporate managements anticipate—even if without pleasure—that some form of social audit will be required in the relatively near future; and for some corporations that future is already taking shape in the form of SEC disclosure requirements.

Looking at all the evidence, the AICPA Committee on Social Measurement identified the likely future directions corporate social reports will take:

1. Disclosure of social information will ultimately become a regular feature of corporate annual reporting.
2. The method of disclosure will become more standardized—probably as a separate social report or as a separate section of a report containing both financial and social information.
3. The information covered in social reports will also become more standardized. All companies will, at a minimum, include their actions in respect to certain specified areas of social concern.
4. As techniques for making quantitative measurements improve, an increasing amount of quantified information will be presented. However, some purely verbal descriptions may always be expected.
5. Corporations will begin presenting more comparisons —with their own past experience, government standards, and industry norms.[42]

Even should such expectations be fulfilled, a report is not the same thing as an action. If corporations feel obliged to render some form of social accounting, that in itself does not oblige them to adopt any policies or engage in any particular activities susceptible to such accounting.

Nevertheless, a felt obligation to make performance public knowledge, particularly under careful guidelines, would almost certainly affect the corporate behavior being reported: "Disclosure offers to business the best chance to demonstrate deeds as well as rhetoric, to recapture the faith of the public and to show its capacity to illuminate the problems and work within the marketplace constraints toward their solution."[43] Actually, statements of this type may not only offer a chance but impose a pressure as well. In Linowes's view, "Socio-economic measurement and reporting, nationally standardized, could exert a sufficiently strong influence on corporate policy to take the built-in payoff out of social irresponsibility."[44]

Back to Motivation

If a corporate social audit is unlikely ever to attain comprehensiveness or be reduceable, by a common denominator, to a bottom line figure or index number, then the question of what corporate social programs are included in the social audit becomes critical in a society that accepts the need for priorities. Here the national plan, with its accompanying social indicators, ties into the corporate social audit:

> Until national goals have been established and national social indicators set, the corporation must mainly rely on an intelligent assessment of the individual social impacts of its business activities and some guidance from interested citizens groups.
>
> Once national goals and indicators have been developed it will be a different set of circumstances. Then as experience multiplies, social indicators will operate much the same as economic and fiscal indicators operate today with regard to economic and corporate policy goals.[45]

Companies whose social performance coincided most effectively with public objectives might be rewarded with preferential credit or tax treatment or with government contracts, as I suggested in the preceding chapter. Eli Goldston, writing before the concept of a corporate social audit had advanced very far, foresaw the possibilities:

> A novel method of incentive and control might be to require expansion of the simple profit scoreboard of business to include an annual public accounting of its performance in other directions: growth in minority group employees, reduction in pollution, improvement in safety records, or encouragement of employees to use mass transportation. In some areas the competitive team spirit of American business might be enough by itself. . . . In other cases economic incentives could be scaled to these achievements, and companies could be given rewards for high grades on the scoreboard in integrated employment and minimal pollution. With these built-in rewards, security analysts should be on the watch for firms with high marks of this kind, recognizing that these companies are working toward compensation for the costs of clean air and clean water, which are too often hidden now. There are also ways to educate the public about the costs of these desirable and necessary activities.[46]

A satisfactory definition of responsible corporate action depends, at least in some instances, on prior definition of social objectives. For example, a company paying high wages might, from a parochial point of view, be regarded as a desirable citizen: what community wants a tightfisted employer? But in times of inflation, above-average wage increases could be regarded as antisocial from the perspective of the nation as a whole. Standards built into a national plan would guide the individual company, bolster receptivity among employees, and win public approval and possibly advantageous future relations with government. To achieve these results, however, wage guidelines would have to be set in a more general policy context. In effect, the corporate social audit (whatever form it ultimately takes), along with more traditional measures of corporate economic operations, would show the respects in which a company had played its part in the overall social design.

Notes

1. Raymond A. Bauer, "The Corporate Social Audit: Getting on the Learning Curve," *California Management Review* 16 (Fall 1973):5.
2. Ibid., p. 6.

3. American Institute of Certified Public Accountants, Committee on Social Measurement, *The Measurement of Corporate Social Performance* (New York: AICPA, 1977), pp. 6–7; hereafter AICPA, *Measurement.*

4. *Corporate Social Reporting in the United States and Western Europe,* report of the Task Force on Corporate Social Performance, U.S. Department of Commerce (Washington, D.C.: GPO, July 1979), p. 12; hereafter *Department of Commerce Report.*

5. John J. Corson and George A. Steiner, *Measuring Business's Social Performance: The Corporate Social Audit* (New York: Committee for Economic Development), pp. 40–41.

6. Ibid., p. 34.

7. John Humble, *Social Responsibility Audit* (London: Foundation for Business Responsibilities, 1973), p. 18.

8. General Informational letter from Homer E. Moyer, Jr., Co-chairman, Task Force on Corporate Social Performance, U.S. Department of Commerce, Washington, D.C., February 1978.

9. David F. Linowes, *The Corporate Conscience* (New York: Hawthorn, 1974), p. 40.

10. AICPA, *Measurement,* p. 6.

11. *Department of Commerce Report,* p. 13.

12. James Traub, "Drawing the Shades on Social Performance," *MBA,* June–July 1978, p. 41.

13. AICPA, *Measurement,* p. 15.

14. Linowes, *The Corporate Conscience,* p. 12.

15. Ibid., p. 13.

16. Corson and Steiner, *Measuring Business's Social Performance,* pp. 57–58.

17. AICPA, *Measurement,* p. 16.

18. *Department of Commerce Report,* p. 13.

19. Letter from Stanley G. Karson, director of the Clearinghouse on Corporate Social Responsibility, Washington, D.C., November 30, 1976, accompanying the 1976 report.

20. Stanley G. Karson, "A 'Social Index' for Business," *Response* (Washington: Clearinghouse on Corporate Social Responsibility, November 1977), p. 2.

21. AICPA, *Measurement,* p. 18.

22. David F. Linowes, "Let's Get On with the Social Audit: A Specific Proposal," *Business and Society Review* No. 4 (Winter 1972–1973): 39–41.

23. *Social Measurement and Reporting* (Philadelphia: Human Resources Network, May 5, 1978), p. 3.

24. Daniel Gray, *One Way to Go about Inventing Social Accounting* (Cambridge: Arthur D. Little Co., Inc., 1973), p. 2.

25. Raymond Bauer, "The State of the Art of Social Auditing" (Harvard Graduate School of Public Administration, November 1972), p. 21.

26. Raymond Bauer, "Commentary," *Business and Society Review* No. 4 (Winter 1972–1973):44.

27. *Department of Commerce Report*, p. 95.
28. AICPA, *Measurement*, p. 16.
29. Corson and Steiner, *Measuring Business's Social Performance*, p. 53.
30. Irwin L. Gubman, secretary of BankAmerica corporation, "Strengthening Public Confidence in Business through Voluntary Disclosure and Codes of Conduct," *Department of Commerce Report*, pp. 39–55.
31. AICPA, *Measurement*, p. 244.
32. *Department of Commerce Report*, pp. 16–17.
33. Corson and Steiner, *Measuring Business's Social Performance*, pp. 62–63.
34. Linowes, "Let's Get On With the Social Audit," p. 41.
35. AICPA, *Measurement*, p. 251.
36. Corson and Steiner, *Measuring Business's Social Performance*, p. 37.
37. SEC Release no. 33-574, May 6, 1976.
38. Bevis Longstreth in a panel discussion, "Corporate Responsibility Panel: The Role of the SEC," *Business Lawyer* 28 (March 1973):231, with citations of several proposals.
39. Ibid., p. 229.
40. Phillip A. Loomis, Jr., in a panel discussion, "Corporate Responsibility Panel: The Role of the SEC," *Business Lawyer* 28 (March 1973):233.
41. Linowes, *The Corporate Conscience*, p. 60.
42. AICPA, *Measurement*, p. 236.
43. Longstreth, "Corporate Responsibility Panel," p. 231.
44. Linowes, *The Corporate Conscience*, p. 61.
45. Ibid, p. 101.
46. Eli Goldston, "New Prospects for American Business," *Daedalus*, Winter 1969, p. 93.

6

Corporate Structure

The present investigation started from the premise that pressures are building on the large corporation requiring it not only to take increased account of its actual social impact but also to make a more searching assessment of its potential social contribution. In the traditional view the social role of a business enterprise is solely to produce goods wanted by consumers at prices competitive with those of other producers; the only test of corporate success in fulfilling that role is profit position. This picture still prevails as far as the operations of a small enterprise go. The small enterprise, too, has its social impact, but the impact is too slight to warrant concern. The small enterprise is called on, by regulatory law and ruling, to meet certain standards of working conditions, product quality in terms of safety and health considerations, pollution control, and so on, but as long as the company complies with the law it is relatively unconstrained by public opinion or pressure.

Not so the large corporation, which has itself become a political entity. However much it might prefer to go about its business and be let alone, the big corporation operates on too large a scale to deserve that privilege. For one thing, its production processes require more structuring and control to achieve the necessary integration of a system depending on many specialized parts. The consequence is to impose greater conformity of performance on each category of workers, at the same time denying them a sense of relationship to the end product. The job itself loses intrinsic significance as well as social significance—the latter an overworked phrase but still trenchant. Large-scale production extrudes not only goods but also people. The catchphrase "quality of working life" seems likely to acquire at least as much significance as "product quality," an outcome that on reflection would not be surprising.

The large corporation affects the communities it penetrates in ways that a small entrepreneur does not. The numbers of people dependent on it for jobs, indirectly as well as directly, its contribution to civic financing, the way it shapes the physical contours and traffic patterns of the locality, its effect on the natural environment—these and still other, more subtle consequences give the big company a special presence in the community. Indeed, the national corporate organization endows the branch office with power often overshadowing that of the host community. Such power, combined with the similar power of other large corporations, affects the economic health of the nation as a whole. Decisions to curtail, maintain, or expand operations have both an immediate impact and a longer term effect on culture, shaping it to reinforce the corporations' position—not the position of the individual company as such but of the corporation as institution. The consumer culture we know today, however one reacts to it, scarcely would have achieved its hold without the influence of the large corporation pursuing profit through production. The advertising profession, which the historian David Potter ranked as one of the great culture molding institutions, along with education and religion, has had its greatest impact with respect not to individual products as much as to the total atmosphere of inducement to consume and the adaptation of the major media to this end.

There is no need for extending the familiar catalogue of ways in which the large corporation, as an institutional phenomenon, *necessarily* has a profound social effect simply in the process of pursuing its own business. No matter how much it would like to separate the social from the business, so that it could disavow the one while holding steadfast to the other, the two come indissolubly united. This unavoidable social impact of the large corporation is now bringing demands for shaping corporate conduct to take account of that influence. Such demands challenge the profit goal, heretofore paramount to the enterprise considered as an economic entity.

Challenging the profit goal also challenges the private property character of the large corporation by asserting a social function that overrides the private property interest, relegating it to a subordinate status.

It would be a considerable exaggeration to say that this result has already materialized, but nonbusiness analysts as well as business leaders have identified this trend. Insofar as corporate management hopes to maintain a leading institutional role in the changing world, it seems incumbent on management to give serious thought to the need for a new corporate strategy—a *social* strategy that not only accommodates but builds on the changing circumstances. And from that premise follows the conclusion that a change in corporate structure is needed to carry out the new strategy. In previous chapters I have attempted to identify tendencies in the direction of a revised corporate strategy and structure. This chapter pulls together these developments in an effort to suggest their implications.

Reorganization at the Top

Let us start with the board of directors, where control is presumed to lie. If there is to be an effective overseeing of executive authority, the board must be responsible for selecting top management, for approving in broad outline the major policy directions, and for monitoring the corporation's performance. These tasks involve a considerable reversal of the present relationship, in which directors are usually named by management and provided with selected information submitted by staff responsible to management. If the social role of the corporation is to expand, then directors must have a broader-than-business perspective. Public directors would seem to be appropriate for all corporations over some specified size. Their qualifications and manner of appointment are obviously matters for discussion. Initial appointments might be made by a college of corporate electors consisting of respected citizens representative either of a cross section of the population or of major social institutions. Conceivably a special government commission might be charged with this function. The SEC has sometimes been suggested, but it scarcely seems the appropriate agency in view of its traditional linkage to investor interests.

Public directors would be appointed for a term, perhaps renewable once. Replacements might come by rotation from other boards or by nomination from the members of the corporate board itself, subject to approval by the initial appointive authority. Public directors would be expected to spend a substantial amount of their time on corporate affairs, perhaps no less than one-quarter time and possibly full-time. Their reviewing function would proceed largely through committees reporting to the full board.

To avoid conflicts of interest members of management would not be eligible for board membership. Fears have sometimes been expressed that "reliance [whether exclusive or not] on 'public interest' directors raises the problems of an adversarial relationship between the board and management,"[1] but this situation is far from inevitable. Whatever strategy managers were selected to carry out, social or other, their objective would presumably be in line with the goals of the board that appointed them. And accountability by itself need not create an adversarial relation. If such a relation did emerge it would more likely result from personality differences. In any event, accountability of executive officers in any organization cannot be dispensed with unless one is ready to move to an authority whose only legitimacy is that which it confers on itself.

Members of management, and especially the chief executive officer, would meet frequently with the board. A close working relationship between the board, as final authority, and management, as initiator and executor of major programs, should enable the board to feel comfortable with its responsibilities without obtruding into management's appropriate areas of discretion by second-guessing decisions implementing major policies previously agreed on. Representatives of other interest groups—shareholders, employees, consumers, environmentalists—would have an opportunity to be heard on matters of broad policy but, of course, would not be entitled to board membership in a representative capacity.

Corporate Relation to National Policy

A corporate social strategy would involve a two-way relation between the board and some national agency defining national policy. The national policy would specify economic priorities and provide inducements to corporations to pursue these goals within the framework of a loose national plan that did not aim at comprehensiveness. Social priorities, indicating social goals whose realization lay within the competence of at least some corporations, would likewise be identified. The composition and authority of the planning agency and its relation to the legislative and executive branches of government could take any of several forms reflecting various pragmatic and ideological compromises.

National planning would include input from institutionalized representatives of the private corporations—perhaps both directors and managers—but this representation would be with respect to the achievement of operating goals, not the pecuniary interests of shareholders. A number of business leaders and at least one business association already have spoken on behalf of the need for a more collaborative relation between government and business, not simply in the sense of understanding each other better but in an operational sense. Such collaboration is desirable as long as its terms are designed for public rather than private interests or, at a minimum, for private interests only to the extent that they serve public interests.

The national economic plan and social indicators would constitute a major factor in a company's definition of its own strategy, a strategy no longer geared singularly to ownership interests but to the corporation's own estimate of how it could best relate operations to the multiple objectives sought, among which would be a net but not a maximum profit. The identification of national economic and social priorities would require a corporate board of (public) directors to face outward with respect to the discharge of board responsibilities. The presumption would be that an exceptionally high rate of return would represent a less than desirable attention to public objectives. An exceptionally low rate of return would normally represent poor management rather than excessive concern for costly social programs since a judicious choice of the latter would pay off in tangible rewards such as preferential credit or tax treatment or beneficial government contracts.

Strategic Planning

The corporation's strategic planning would require the board to face inward, establishing the linkage between national social and corporate social objectives. The latter could be effectively laid out in broad terms only in close consultation with top management. Once decided, such goals would be management's responsibility to carry out; management would report frequently to the board, which would refrain from interference as long as management actions lay within the broad outlines agreed on and were executed in a way that carried no actual threat to the corporation's security.

In order to protect management's sphere of discretion from board intrusion, major corporate objectives (settled on after full discussion between board and management) should be spelled out with enough specificity to permit reasonable judgment as to whether they are being realized in the more detailed strategic and operating plans that it is management's duty to elaborate and in the operations flowing from such plans. The importance of this major link in the chain running from board to top management to the overall corporate organization requires attention to the planning process.

> Corporate planning is normally, or nominally, a process which commits the subordinate units of the enterprise to achieve certain objectives which are specified for varying periods of time, from the immediate present to a future distant by five years or more. The commitment may be affirmative, acquiescent, or imposed, depending on whether the subordinate unit has sufficient discretion to feel that its part in the plan has been reached by agreement with its superior, or whether plans for the unit have been made for it though it is accorded the privilege of commenting on the result (with assent expected), or whether its role has been handed to it to play without further discussion. Regardless of the degree of commitment by the parts to the whole, however, the plan—at least in most large corporations—is intended to tie together all phases of the company's activity in an integrated effort to achieve identified goals.[2]

When I wrote the preceding paragraph some twenty years ago, I considered a *profit target* to be the primary objective of the large firm even though I recognized secondary goals. The profit target was pursued through a comprehensive budget, broken down to the lowest operating units. The budget objectives for each unit in effect constituted surrogates for their part of the overall corporate objective:

> Because the relation of their contribution to the over-all design is frequently obscure to supervisors and employees in subordinate levels, the lower the unit in the organizational hierarchy, the more does the plan—the budget—stand as surrogate for the objective itself, so that "making budget" becomes the goal, instead of—as at higher levels in the business—the ends for which the budget simply stands as means. As a consequence, the importance

97

of the budget in integrating all phases of a company's activities and at all levels of its operations is joined by its importance in providing a set of generally understood and (frequently) accepted standards on the strength of which any unit's performance can be judged. This dual aspect of the comprehensive budget makes it an instrument of such significance to the enterprise that only top management can make it effective.[3]

This view of the planning-budgeting process in the large corporation probably still obtains today. Its applicability to a future when a different corporate strategy may motivate the large corporation requires only a slight reinterpretation of words but a major reinterpretation of intent. Obviously, the chief change would be in the prime objective: no longer would all other goals be secondary to a profit target set in light of profit *potential* and by which plan realization was measured; no longer would departures from plan—favorable or unfavorable—be measured only by revenue and cost variances, with plan revisions and operating changes made accordingly. In the new scheme, the target rate of return would be set *in relation to* such other principal goals as a contribution to specific national economic objectives. Though profitable, activities of this nature might not earn as high a profit as endeavors having a lower social priority. Social objectives, less definable in economic terms but often involving a cost (even if only the cost of a performance review), would sacrifice cost efficiency and hence full profit potential. How much less a profit would be acceptable would be a policy decision to be made by the board of directors in consultation with management.

The shift in emphasis, then, is in how the corporation would conceive of the profit target in its planning—whether (as now) as the realization of as much of its profit potential as seemed feasible under all existing or foreseen circumstances or (as under a social strategy) as the realization of a profit that seemed consonant with both corporate continuity and overall goal realization. In reflecting on the magnitude of this change, one should keep in mind the underlying premise of a prior shift in motivation, precipitated by irresistible public and political pressures, whose accommodation may be necessary to the survival of the private corporation as an institution ("private" in this context refers not to private property but to private initiative and discretion).

In the preparation of the short-run operating plan (and to a somewhat lesser extent in drafting the longer run strategic plan) it would be important to involve as many organizational personnel as possible. To the extent that the corporation made its overall goals known to and understood by all its people, down to the lowest paid employee, the more likely it would be to elicit a contributing effort on their part—especially in the case of goals clearly geared to social advantage rather than to shareholders' return or to targeted profit standing alone.

Participation in Planning and Execution

Broad participation in a general promulgation of goals should go hand in hand with the involvement of managers at all levels in the planning process itself and especially in the identification of results for which they and their units will be held accountable. In the act of participating the subunit imposes on itself a commitment; all such commitments, taken together, rationalize the total plan.

Again, it is worth comparing present and possible future procedures. Consider this 1960 statement from an official of a Massachusetts company:

> The Company believes strongly in the principle that for budgeting to be effective it must be done at all levels by the people who are responsible for the operation of the Company. Consequently, each of the divisions of the Company prepares its own budget which, after review and approval by management, are consolidated to give the overall Company budgets. . . . To ensure a reasonable degree of consistency, certain major premises on which the budget is built are agreed upon and issued to the divisions.[4]

If we substitute for the words "budgeting" and "budget" the words "planning" and "plan," recognizing the latter as incorporating the former but no longer related solely to a profit target, the foregoing statement could apply when a company's objectives were expanded.

Of course, it is too much to expect that such participatory planning can be carried off effectively in all large corporations—perhaps even in *any* large corporation. The demands on individuals and organization may be excessive, so that the procedure represents at best an ideal. Even in some companies that now make a fetish of supervisory participation in planning, preliminary unit objectives are at times prepared by the controller's office or the accounting department for approval or suggested modification by the supervisor. Nevertheless, there is considerable merit in providing each supervisor with an opportunity to be heard before his part of the plan is written into the whole. Such a hearing may convert what otherwise would be an imposed task into a personal commitment.

Plan implementation, like formulation, benefits from close attention to discretion and participation at all levels. Whatever decisions are made affecting the organization's realization of goals, the decisionmakers should be encouraged to interact with others, both inside and outside the corporation, whose opinions or assistance would be helpful—always with the proviso that such relations must not compromise other overall corporate objectives or the actions of other units in helping to realize them. The intent is to stimulate people at all levels, particularly those with managerial responsibilities, to consider impact on the environment, for example, as much as production efficiency; to concern themselves with product design for consumer safety (within the limits of their authority) as much as design for sales appeal; and to involve themselves with improving the quality of working life as much as with improving technical capability.

Motivation

If corporate policy is genuinely to be broadened to incorporate social objectives on the same plane as profit objectives, such a change in motivation cannot be accomplished simply by locating appropriately titled officials at high levels within the organization, say, a vice-president for environmental affairs or a director of community relations. Establishing such staff functions, without making additional adjustments, may simply absolve operating personnel from further concern with the substance of decisions in these areas. Staff supervision has its place, but actual responsibility must go right down to the operating manager. Just as that manager must now concern himself with production schedules and financial efficiency (in the form of cost control) and product (marketing) quality, so he also must concern himself with the social objectives his operations affect.

In order to give credibility to the seriousness with which top management viewed this enlarged responsibility, an appropriate incentive system might be introduced. In the first instance, incentives might take the form of added remuneration. International Paper, for example, now includes in its overall planning and budgeting procedures a

> method for setting business-oriented goals and for measuring performance in areas such as public issues which do not fit specifically into the traditional functions of finance, manufacturing, or marketing. [These are labeled "budgeted nonfinancial objectives."] "Budgeted" because they are an integral part of the short- and long-term planning and review process. "Non-Financial" because they need not be measured in financial terms, or even in quantifiable terms, but still require action in the social, technological, and governmental areas.[5]

Donald Brennan, executive vice-president of International Paper, commented:

> The effectiveness of the process, to a great extent, depends on management's performance being tied directly, or at least in significant part, to the system by which management is compensated. If the corporation is to be credible, it can only become so through the accomplishments of its managers. Therefore, management behavior on an individual basis must be changed. And for behavior to change, internal values must change. The best method we have devised so far to accomplish this behavioral change is to relate performance on Budgeted Non-Financial Objectives to management's reward—that is, to its compensation. In 1976, for example, approximately 50 percent of the incentive compensation award paid to International Paper managers was based on performance on Budgeted Non-Financial Objectives. In other words, BNFO is a process for establishing new value systems within the corporation. Non-financial goals are treated as equal in importance to financial goals, thereby institutionalizing their significance to the corporation as well as to individual managers.[6]

It is no discredit to International Paper to observe that such socially responsible behavior has limits (as Brennan himself admitted) related to the economic goals of the business, which in the present private competitive system must still be geared chiefly to profit performance. Under the circumstances, pecuniary incentives are understandable. But if the time should come when a corporation's actions are to be motivated by considerations other than profit potential, it may become desirable to provide nonpecuniary incentives (or, perhaps more correctly, additional incentives) to encourage the change in internal values Brennan mentioned. Added responsibility, with promotion based on overall good performance, may be one of the most potent of such tools—not only because of higher pay, though of course that feature would play a part, but also because of institutional recognition of a form of public service.

The difficulties in adapting as complex an organization as the large business corporation to such a modified framework of operations cannot be dismissed. There would, of course, be enormous resistance from most people who had attained positions of authority under the present corporate system. Nevertheless, younger people entering on business careers are likely to have less difficulty in accepting—even welcoming—the restructured corporation. Göran Ohlin suggested, from Swedish experience, what might also occur in the United States:

> The task of reconciling the many and conflicting interests that converge on a company is becoming an increasingly difficult managerial function. . . . But the mood among young executives is not one of despondency. On the contrary, one often encounters an almost exuberant pride among managers who feel capable of meeting their new responsibilities toward all interested parties—employees, customers, stockholders, and community—without renouncing their competitive strength. Such men tend to be impatient with the perennial grumbling about the new rules of the game on the part of the trade associations and other business organizations, which seem to many of the young to be fighting a sterile rearguard action against the course of history.[7]

Moreover, the shift in corporate role may mean that jobs provide greater satisfaction than they now offer. In recent years sociologists have discovered that many workers, especially younger workers, feel alienated from their jobs—another term that has been overworked to the point of dullness but without destroying its validity. The specialized task by itself may have little interest, the product to which it is tributary may be trivial, the purpose of the whole operation—a rate of return—may be totally unrelated to the activities of most workers. The shift to corporate responsibility for identified social objectives might endow at least some positions with a significance now lacking.

Performance Review

No plan, however well conceived and motivated, executes itself; hence there is a need for performance review to see if the plan is on target and if not, why not. A corporate social strategy requires a corporate social audit. The latter's design should be in part the board's prerogative, taking into its own hands the specification of the flows of information that it believes necessary to determine how well the company is meeting goals. To this end, the board may request fuller information in certain areas. For example, following Christopher Stone's suggestion, the board of an automobile company might have special concern about the safety record of a newly designed model, or the board of a pharmaceutical company about a new drug, and they might call for information from sources that normally are not tapped (repair garages, private practitioners).[8] In matters like these, the private corporation can use ingenuity and call on its own facilities to meet recognized social responsibilities and in the process perhaps avoid governmental regulatory overload.

But performance review and social audit are also vital to top management to enable it to judge how closely all parts of the organization are meeting their respective commitments, which add up to the overall performance wanted. Such a review would identify areas of actual or potential difficulty, just as is the case now when there are variances from budget; with a plan enlarged to incorporate social objectives, the elements of such a review would be more diverse, as we saw in examining the social audit, and the manner of making appropriate adjustments to bring plan and performance into conformity would require greater flexibility and inventiveness. What would be involved, then, is both an ongoing reporting system, disclosing primarily for management's benefit the short-term (perhaps weekly or monthly, certainly quarterly) relation between plan and activity, and a periodic audit (perhaps quarterly, certainly annually) providing a more summary statement for the benefit of board and management.

In this model, the reporting system runs through the company, paralleling the organizational structure; each unit renders an account, encompassing the results from all subunits under its jurisdiction. The significance of deviations from plan depends in part on the level of authority of the manager who reviews such discrepancies. From the standpoint of the manager in whose unit the variance occurs, inability to "make plan" requires explanation and extra effort. From the standpoint of higher authority, however, variances at some point may invite replanning a major phase of the company's operations or even the totality of its operations.

Of course, actual performance may be expected to deviate somewhat from plan, necessitating regular adjustments between planning and action. Nevertheless, at any given time *some* plan, whether original or revised, exists by which the performance of all organizational units, as well as the corporation as a whole, can be judged and deviations from which signal the need for either further control or further revision. Management and board must determine whether adverse variances can be corrected and favorable deviations consolidated to permit retention and eventual accomplishment of the original objectives or whether the variances are caused by circumstances sufficiently unmanageable to require a new plan, usually less desirable on paper than the original but likely to achieve better results in the execution.

This is, in fact, the model of the planning-budgeting system at the present time, geared to a profit target. It would remain the model under a new corporate social strategy except for the extended reporting and the greater variety of adjustments required to deal with variances. However, these additional considerations are not likely to be trivial. Reporting on performance with respect to social objectives would sometimes, perhaps often, have to be made in qualitative terms, which lend themselves more readily to obfuscation—either to make the reporting unit look good or to absolve the responsible superior of blame for lack of accomplishment (one analyst referred to the latter motive as a "shared feeling on the part of subordinate officials that they owe their loyalty chiefly to senior management and not to the board"[9]). To overcome this weakness corporations must try to inculcate a greater sense of social obligation in each reporting unit, reflecting the changed objectives of the corporation as an entity; to improve methods of reporting on social programs whose results cannot be quantified; and—in the end—to rely on periodic audits, both internal and external, as checks on performance.

Proxy Machinery and Annual Meetings

Without attempting a comprehensive overview of other structural changes that might be required to further the revised corporate strategy, it may be noted that the proxy machinery as it now exists would no longer be relevant and could be dismantled. Since the status of the large corporation as the private property of its shareholders would have been given up, there would be no need for securing their approval (even as pro forma as it is now) of directors or external auditors or resolutions. It might be considered desirable for shareholders to designate some agent to represent their interests to the board, and for such a purpose something akin to the proxy system, run by a stockholders' "union" rather than by the corporation itself, might be appropriate.

Similarly, an annual meeting of shareholders, to which the board and management reported, would lose its significance. On the other hand, a public annual meeting at which directors and managers would report and submit to questioning on their stewardship and activities would seem very much in order. Such a meeting probably would resemble a press conference and undoubtedly would generate greater public attention than do shareholders' meetings, corporate press releases, and other devices currently used.

External Monitoring

Earlier I referred to the need for a check on actual corporate performance, particularly in the areas of social concern where, at least initially, lack of experience in reporting would make practice imperfect. Such a corporate social audit, for reasons set out in the preceding chapter, should be both internal and external, but the external check would be of special importance if the organizational arrangements touched on here should materialize. If some version of a loosely integrated plan identifying national economic priorities should be developed, along with a system of indicators of desired social policies capable of being furthered by corporate initiatives, and if corporations were to be given preferred treatment on the basis of accomplishments in the designated areas, then some means of certifying those accomplishments would be essential. I turn next to that issue.

Notes

1. John Coffee, "Beyond the Shut-eyed Sentry: Toward a Theoretical View of Corporate Misconduct and an Effective Legal Response," *Virginia Law Review* 63 (November 1977):1145.
2. Neil W. Chamberlain, *The Firm: Micro-economic Planning and Action* (New York: McGraw-Hill, 1962), p. 294.

3. Ibid, p. 295.
4. Ibid., p. 81.
5. *Corporate Social Reporting in the United States and Western Europe,* U.S. Department of Commerce (Washington, D.C.: G.P.O., July 1979), pp. 150–151.
6. Idem.
7. Göran Ohlin, "The Changing Role of Private Enterprise in Sweden," in Karl H. Cerny (ed.), *Scandinavia at the Polls* (Washington, D.C.: American Enterprise Institute for Public Policy Research, 1977), p. 263.
8. Christopher Stone, *Where the Law Ends* (New York: Harper & Row, 1975), p. 203.
9. Coffee, "Beyond the Shut-eyed Sentry," p. 1131.

7

The Monitoring Professions

"The professional is no longer sure just who his client is. And those who must use professionals to sort through the regulatory maze are discovering that 'their' lawyer or accountant has become society's policeman."[1] *Business Week* thus summed up one of the major problems confronting the "troubled professions." The professions in greatest trouble are accounting and law. One analyst raised the question whether a corporation's outside counsel and auditors, like its directors, are "becoming increasingly responsible to the public at large, rather than to the corporate entity or to the shareholders of any given moment."[2]

But new professions may also be in the process of being created to serve as society's watchdogs—professionals employed by business but responsible to the public. In 1979 a representative of the Environmental Protection Agency's enforcement office suggested the possibility of environmental auditors—specialists licensed by the agency but hired by the corporation to monitor air and water quality and waste discharges. Their findings would be made public, just as publicly held corporations release financial reports prepared by outside "public" auditors. "The only way we are going to be able to monitor all polluters is through the use of the private sector," William Robinson of the EPA commented.[3] Comparable checks on industrial applications of scientific findings also have been proposed.[4]

Accounting

This chapter is concerned only with accounting and legal professionals, chiefly the former. The large public accounting firms have been in the spotlight. As a distinguished professor of accounting noted, auditors are exposed to "essential demands of society for the auditors' assurances of complete visibility and accountability from our major corporations."[5] Another eminent professor of accounting reported that "attempts are being made to give the independent auditor either a separate role in [corporate] governance or a cooperative one with the board of directors and audit committees."[6]

Leading practitioners in the accounting profession have recognized this development. Clifford Graese, partner of Peat, Marwick, Mitchell and Company, observed that "some segments of the public" are applying

> pressure to auditors to take on added responsibilities not only to prevent, or disclose, improper payments but also to establish (as in the case of financial statements) some guidelines for distinguishing between proper and improper practices and disclosures. . . . The public is looking to the auditing profession to help develop and enforce a stronger discipline in protecting and in disclosing improper activity.[7]

As Norman Auerbach, chairman of Coopers & Lybrand, testified to a U.S. Senate subcommittee:

> The public and the courts . . . want us to do more, and clearly they want us to take on greater responsibility for what we do. The decision as to whether we choose to do more is not within our control. The decision as to whether we will step up to these increased responsibilities is not within our control. Not any more. We *must* be responsive.[8]

The periodic audit of a corporation's financial accounts by an independent agency traditionally has aimed to provide

> a substantial measure of confidence to investors and creditors that their funds can be entrusted with reasonable security to the management of the corporation. . . . The quality of audited financial statements and the image they convey of a corporation have had great influence over the ability to raise money and thus have gov-

erned the mobilization and flow of enormous amounts of capital into business enterprise.[9]

In performing the auditing role, the accounting profession works within a structure built up over the years but modified in minor ways. Financial data are organized and presented by management and reviewed by the auditor (a certified public accountant) in accordance with generally accepted rules (GAAP). Nevertheless, considerable judgment must be exercised. The financial review normally concludes: "In our opinion the financial statements present fairly the financial position of the company and the results of its operations in conformity with generally accepted principles consistently applied during the period." Although "the opinion was never intended to be a 'good housekeeping seal of approval,' " Geoffrey Chalmers noted, "unavoidably, it has gained that position in the mind of the public."[10]

The corporate audit was recognized as of sufficient importance in providing investors with confidence in a company's integrity that the 1933 federal securities legislation accorded the new Securities and Exchange Commission power to prescribe the form of accounts, the details to be shown in the balance sheet and earning statement, and methods to be followed in the preparation of the accounts. Instead of undertaking these responsibilities solely on its own, the SEC moved toward an arrangement with the principal professional association in the field, the American Institute of Accountants, subsequently the American Institute of Certified Public Accountants, through the institute's Accounting Principles Board. In 1972 the latter, which had been controlled by part-time practitioners and had been viewed as an appendage of the association that had spawned it, was replaced by a more independent Financial Accounting Standards Board (FASB), whose seven members, all serving five-year terms and three of whom need not be CPAs, must suspend professional practice during their tenure: "Although not so stated, presumably one reason for creating a board completely divorced from practice was to assure maximum independence and thereby end the suspicion that accounting firm representatives on the Accounting Principles Board sometimes voted according to preferences of clients rather than their own convictions."[11]

However, the SEC has never surrendered to a private sector agency its authority over accounting practices:

> Through the Office of the Chief Accountant, the Commission indicates which accounting or auditing problems it considers most

pressing. In some cases . . . the Commission has virtually dictated immediate action by the FASB. More often, however, the Commission suggests its areas of interest informally or approves the topics being considered by the private bodies. As pronouncements are formulated by the FASB or the AICPA, drafts are reviewed in detail with members of the Commission staff, whose views receive high priority. Generally speaking, pronouncements are not issued without the blessing of the SEC staff.[12]

In the course of an audit, disagreements over the interpretation of principles frequently arise between a company's management and its independent auditors, who may then jointly consult SEC staff:

In such cases, the SEC staff tends to place both reliance and obligations on the independent auditor. The staff will not always accept an accounting interpretation which has been agreed to by both management and the independent auditor, but it will almost never approve accounting which is not proposed, or at least accepted, by the independent auditor.[13]

The auditor's independence of management—his ability to serve as an objective monitor—cannot help but remain a continuing issue. For one thing, the AICPA, the chief professional association, takes the official position that "the accounts of a company are primarily the responsibility of management. The responsibility of the auditor is to express his opinion concerning the financial statements and to state clearly such explanations, amplifications, disagreements, or disapproval as he deems appropriate."[14] Since commonly there is no one principle that alone is appropriate to a particular situation, the role the accounting profession sees for itself is to certify that the principles selected by management are appropriate and have some precedent either in prior practice (the company's own or others') or in the literature: "An accountant may certify a statement even though he believes that the principles employed in its preparation do not account for the underlying transactions as fairly as competing principles that management has rejected."[15] This latitude has been somewhat narrowed by an AICPA ruling that makes it unethical for a member to certify to the acceptability of financial statements that actually depart from an accounting principle promulgated by the FASB in a way that distorts the meaning of the statements taken as a whole. The significance of this ruling, while real, is lessened by the fact that FASB standards do not cover all situations, are necessarily incomplete and sometimes vague, and lend themselves to variant interpretations: "As long as management rather than the accountant is empowered to make discretionary choices among competing accounting principles [or interpretations], such choices will often lack soundness and will invariably lack objectivity."[16]

The possibility that in a difference of opinion over the appropriateness of accounting principles or their interpretation management is likely to have the deciding voice is reinforced by the fact that the selection or dismissal of the auditing firm typically lies with management. Melvin Eisenberg summarized succinctly his conclusions regarding the weakness of present auditing procedures:

> It is impossible to expect objective reporting from an institutional structure which combines (1) power of selection of accounting principles by the very managers whose activities are being accounted for, (2) wide discretion in making that selection, and (3) auditing of that selection by persons hired and fired by the very managers who make that selection.[17]

The independence of the external auditor relative to corporate management has been further jeopardized, in the view of Harold Williams, former SEC chairman, because large accounting firms (the "big eight") typically audit the books of a corporation for many years, developing a close, sympathetic, and mutually advantageous relationship with clients.[18]

So vigorous has been the contention that corporate managements dominate the auditing process, on which investors have come to rely as certifying a corporation's integrity, that all the principal parties involved—the accounting profession, corporate managements, and the SEC—have addressed this issue. One approach has been to increase the responsibility of corporate directors for the auditing process so that management has less control over it. The usual means is the creation of an audit committee with special responsibility for reviewing both procedures and results and reporting to the full board. Coopers & Lybrand, one of the major accounting firms, has for some years urged establishment of board audit committees and (along with some other firms) has published guidelines for such committees:

> Independence of the auditor exists to the extent that the auditor is able and willing to disagree with management should the occasion

arise. This sense of independence can be generated through an active audit committee consisting of members of the board of directors. Such an audit committee—which should comprise only non-management outside directors—should be responsible for hiring and firing the auditor.

The committee should assess and judge the objectivity of the relationship between auditor and management. In addition, the committee should review the scope and quality of all services provided by the auditor.[19]

Elaborating on the duties of such a committee:

> The audit committee should be an activist group in the sense of approving the audit schedule, participating in setting audit policy, being apprised of major findings, and overseeing the coordination of internal and external audit operations. In order for the audit committee to assume this role, it should be involved in the annual establishment of the internal audit schedule.[20]

Although "the accounting profession has repeatedly recommended audit committees,"[21] the AICPA has resisted the SEC's suggestion that it adopt a professional standard requiring that any publicly held corporation serviced by one of its members have such a committee. The New York Stock Exchange, on the other hand, has insisted since 1978 that any listed company have an audit committee composed of outside directors. Clearly there has been a strong tendency in support of such an institutional practice.

Nevertheless, an audit committee by itself guarantees nothing. There are questions pertaining to the powers it possesses and how effectively it exercises them. In some instances a committee may have more shadow than substance, constituting a cover for management's continued domination of the audit procedure. In other instances it may encounter noncooperation or even hostility from management:

> The managements of some companies have felt uneasy about the establishment of audit committees and, in some instances, have been resentful of what they consider to be unjust criticism. On occasion, company officials have criticized audit committees for reviewing operational areas and decisions they felt should be left entirely to management.[22]

In 1977, when Grumman's audit committee undertook to investigate payoffs on overseas sales, apparently continuing in blatant defiance of board policy ("so frequent as to raise serious questions concerning the ability of the board to supervise Grumman's business conduct effectively") it met with resistance and ridicule. The president "expressed belief that this committee's investigation was a needless intrusion upon and an interference with Grumman American's sales activities."[23]

Even without facing actual hostility, an audit committee can be relegated to a passive role by a management that dominates the board. The situation at California Life is instructive in this respect. On April 12, 1979, members of the corporation's audit committee learned that the company had not filed with the SEC its 1978 annual financial report, due April 1. The life insurance holding company was at the time embroiled with its independent auditors in an accounting dispute. The SEC denied a request for extension of the filing deadline, but in fact the report was not submitted until August:

> Where was the audit committee during all this conflict? Apparently, it was largely missing in action. In 1978 and the critical early months of 1979, when the dispute arose, the committee held only two rather perfunctory meetings; at least one other was canceled. It made several recommendations but didn't push aggressively for their adoption. Communication with the auditors was practically nil. . . . Some people close to the situation contend that the company's problems couldn't have been avoided. They particularly cite the helplessness of any audit committee faced with headstrong management.[24]

The disagreement between management and auditing firm turned on the former's attempt to defer an "unusually large" amount of so-called indirect costs related to the acquisition of new insurance policies and the audit team's unwillingness to acquiesce, doubting whether the deferred costs could in fact be recovered:

> Until the April 12 meeting, the debate between the company and the auditors raged on without the knowledge or participation of the audit committee, even though Dean Jones, head of the Delotte, Haskins & Sells team, 'discussed with company officers the need to involve the audit committee in the resolution of the year-end audit' as early as March 24, the special report [prepared at the request of the audit committee by special counsel] says. He apparently didn't press the issue until April 11, however. And even after April 12, the committee remained mostly an observer.[25]

The president was said to have expressed the view that deeper involvement of the committee would have shown lack of faith in management. Subsequently the question was raised whether the auditing firm should itself have taken the initiative earlier in bringing the problem to the attention of the audit committee even without management's approval. But a partner of the accounting firm called such a situation "extremely rare," adding "I can think of no case where we bypassed management."[26]

Accounting experts argue that it is the obligation of the audit committee itself to follow audit issues and confer with the auditor. "Directors, however, frequently fear that such assertiveness would upset the genial relationship with management that they find comfortable and necessary to keep the corporate gears well-oiled." As a lawyer representing California Life remarked: "There's a limited amount of time and a lot of ground to cover. The whole atmosphere and protocol of a board meeting makes it difficult to play the role of critic as the SEC envisions." And an outside director commented on the "element of trust among directors," even those on the audit committee. He observed, "If management tells you something, you believe it. Otherwise, you wouldn't be on the board."[27]

Most experts concur that the "audit committee's role is still filled with gray areas and is still evolving":

> How far can or should it go in scrutinizing corporate activities? And is it—as one chief executive warned Conference Board interviewers—gaining too much power?
>
> Such doubts help explain the seemingly passive stance of Cal Life's audit committee. "Who has the supreme wisdom to say he's smarter than the guys who are in there every day?" an audit-committee member asks. "Who would have the omnipotence to tell the managers they're incompetent?"[28]

What this shows, concluded the company lawyer previously cited, is "how easy it is for a conscientious group of outside directors to be soft-soaped by senior management."[29]

Recognizing the potential conflict between management and board over direction and control of the external audit, Eisenberg recommended that the audit committee (composed entirely of independent directors) "have the exclusive power (1) to nominate and recommend dismissal of the corporation's accountant on behalf of the board, and (2) to direct the accountant's activities and set the terms of his engagement."[30] Even these requirements obviously constitute no assurance that the committee will use its powers wisely and well. There is nothing to prevent it from relying—passively—on the auditors it selects and for the same easy relationship of trust (and complacency) to develop among the audit committee, the auditing firm, the board as a whole, and management. Indeed, some observers believe that any other arrangement casts the audit committee and board into a role not unlike that of the private detective, searching for transgressions and assuming responsibility for the moral integrity of management. But the tenor of the times is against a relapse into this former relaxed posture. A raft of proposals for reforms of one sort or another center around the external auditor but necessarily with implications for corporate board and management.

At the most lenient end of the spectrum of reform recommendations are those maintaining it is up to board and management to formulate specific standards of corporate conduct:

> The accountant has no unique philosophical training which enables him to make value judgments . . . or to draw lines of ethical standards any more clearly than any other individual. . . . The principal burden of responsibility for upgrading the standards of corporate behavior must lie with those who make the decisions involved, namely, the corporate executives. . . . A concerted dedication on the part of the board of directors and key executives can and will improve corporate behavior at all levels. The accounting profession can be of help. But most certainly, if the public is looking to the accounting profession as the primary force in correcting ills of the corporate world through policing action, it has failed to recognize the true nature of the problem.[31]

The presiding member of the AICPA Commission on Auditors' Responsibilities, Lee Seidler, would go somewhat further in assigning obligations to external accountants. While it is up to management to choose the accounting principles by which corporate operations are judged, the independent auditor is not thereby absolved from his own professional responsibility:

> Too many auditors believed that so long as the company selected accounting principles and practices which were minimally acceptable, no further guidance was required from the auditor. The Commission on Auditors' Responsibilities emphatically disagreed with this belief. . . .
> The Commission recommended that generally accepted auditing standards should include a requirement that the independent

auditor determine that his client has selected the accounting principles and practices which are "preferable" in the circumstances,
whenever alternatives exist and a rational choice can be made
among them.[32]

Moving further along the spectrum in the direction of assigning
firmer responsibilities to the auditor, Eisenberg concluded:

> Since a major purpose of financial statements is to measure man-
> agement's performance, and since the financial data reported by a
> corporation depend in significant part on discretionary choices
> among competing accounting principles, it is reasonable to expect
> that the principles employed in the preparation of a corporation's
> financial statements will be selected by the corporation's outside
> accountant, and not by its managers. The outside accountant, af-
> ter all, is a professional, skilled in accounting principles and prac-
> tice, and presumably objective in the exercise of his direction. In
> contrast, the manager typically has no advanced training in ac-
> counting and is invariably highly self-interested in selecting those
> principles that show off his performance in the best possible
> light.[33]

One way of relieving the auditor from individual responsibility to
monitor clients—admittedly a tenuous position if management is
free to dismiss him—is to strengthen the general professional standards to which an auditing firm must conform. A number of recommendations for improved self-regulation by the accounting profession have been put forward. In general, they tend to incorporate a
requirement that all CPAs who audit public companies belong to a
special private sector accounting body that would set its own standards, require periodic peer review of all members' procedures, and
exercise disciplinary powers—including expulsion.[34] In fact, a wa-
tered down version of these requirements has emerged. Under the
aegis of the AICPA, an SEC practice section has been established
composed of an executive committee, a peer review committee, and
a five-member public overseer board. Membership in the section is
not mandatory for public corporation auditors, and the part-time
public board lacks direct authority over members.

Both the SEC and the Senate subcommittee that undertook a
critical inquiry into the public accounting profession expressed mis-
givings as to the adequacy of the measures adopted. The Senate
subcommittee staff urged that Congress require the SEC or some
other federal agency to prescribe the rules and standards to be fol-

lowed in auditing public corporations. Reliance on the profession, in effect since 1938, would be abandoned. The SEC proposed that the standard auditor's opinion include an evaluation of the adequacy of the company's internal accounting system.

In this continuing controversy over the responsibility of the external auditor as monitor of corporate financial conduct, one clear intention has been to make the auditor more independent of management. One proposal suggests that accounting firms divest themselves of a variety of management advisory services that are at best peripheral to the accounting function, such as executive recruitment, market analysis, plant layout, and tax advice, on the ground that accounting firms seeking such additional business are more likely to acquiesce in management's wishes. Indeed, criticism directed at the management-auditor relationship has tended to weight the relative bargaining positions of these two in the latter's favor.

Questions remain, however, over what the CPA is bargaining for in his relation with management. What is the CPA going to do with any enhanced independence that may actually be *forced* on him? Here we return to the larger perspective of the present investigation. The end result of airing this prickly question of the role of auditor as corporate monitor may be to make the latter role an essential part of a revised corporate structure premised on a new corporate social strategy. Although Eisenberg's impressive legal study of the structure of corporations was cast essentially within the existing system of shareholder ownership of the corporation, with the obligations of management, board, and auditors framed in that context, he recognized a broader potential: "Although the primary role of the accountant is to audit management's financial results, once the accountants have been made independent they will provide a capability enabling directors to audit management's performance in other areas as well." He mentioned such matters as degree of market penetration, comparative costs, the soundness of a company's capital budgeting procedures, and sales forecasting techniques. "Finally, the capability brought to the board by truly independent accountants would enable it to audit management's results in meeting relevant nonfinancial objectives, such as compliance with law, due respect for the environment, provision of safe working conditions, nondiscrimination, and fair treatment of the consumer."[35] Eisenberg viewed these social concerns as constraints on the private corporation, but they might also be viewed as indicating a far broader potential range of social initiatives, along the lines examined in previous chapters. In that event, the auditor's opinion would cover a greater breadth of corporate activity and be of concern to a larger audience. It would also move beyond matters to which generally accepted or even professionally identified accounting principles could readily be applied. The consequence would be, almost certainly, to rule out the unqualified opinions auditors usually are now able to give.

The AICPA Committee on Social Measurement, in recognizing the foregoing limitation on an audit extended to social programs, asked whether there might be a point intermediate between the unqualified auditor's opinion and an opinion that relied "solely on the word of the person preparing the data." The committee argued that such an intermediate position might be filled by what it termed "review to develop a suitability appraisal" or, for our purposes, simply a "suitability appraisal":

> The suitability appraisal would be the personal opinion of the independent expert vis-à-vis the work of the company, and the appraisal made would be the opinion of one expert or firm. As an individual or even a firm—whether agreeing or disagreeing with the company—the expert's authority would be far less weighty than that which would be derived from broadly supported authoritative standards. . . .
>
> Moving from a single expert's opinion, through a useful degree of consensus, to an "authoritative standard" may take many routes. . . .
>
> An officially promulgated government regulation might be used as the standard for disclosure and reporting for that area. If there were a government regulation specifying all areas of reporting, and indicators within those areas, definitions of terms, and so forth, they could be similarly used. If areas, indicators, and definitions were established by a nongovernment body, or by one in which the government was only one participant, such lists could also be used as standards. They might not be the best, but they would be "authoritative," established independent of the company, and could be amended. A longer, slower, and less certain approach relies on the emergence of a consensus. In any approach, however, research will be required into what things are significant and what information can be provided about them. . . .
>
> As standards and techniques emerge and improve, one can anticipate that the information in an increasing number of areas will become suitable for audit. In the meantime, periodic suitability appraisals can serve the purposes of a corporate management, a special committee of a board of directors or of others concerned

118

with the development of corporate policies and the impact of corporate actions. . . .

It is not unreasonable to assume that the technical difficulties and cost of auditing will place limits on what eventually can and will be audited. Where these limits lie should ultimately be established on the basis of experience gained in carrying out audit examinations and "suitability appraisals" and evidence of the importance attached by society to different degrees of assurance.[36]

A precedent for such an expanded audit exists in the federal government's General Accounting Office. Under congressional prodding, this agency has gone far beyond its original function of financial accounting to check on waste and mismanagement in government programs. The GAO now assesses program as well as managerial effectiveness in an increasing range of government operations. While the GAO has been criticized for overreaching its capability and encroaching on areas of executive authority, its enlarged sphere of responsibility has clearly been of Congress's making in an effort to develop a tool that would assist the legislature "to pull even with the executive branch in setting national policy." In response to charges that the GAO's expertise outside financial accounting is questionable, the office has widened its contacts with experts in other fields and assembled an advisory group to evaluate its own studies.[37] The AICPA committee similarly suggested that although the professionals with the greatest relevant experience in corporate auditing are CPAs, they can be assisted by researchers and practitioners in a variety of fields using social information.

Law

In some respects, corporate lawyers have the same problem as accountants in defining their role vis-à-vis the corporation. Whether inside counsel or outside retained counsel, to whom are they responsible? Do they accept and defend management's interpretation of legal principles unless patently unlawful? Do they, on their own responsibility, protect the interests of corporate constituencies (notably shareholders) in the face of unlawful managerial actions contrary to those interests? Do they have an obligation to disclose to appropriate government authorities unlawful managerial actions harmful to the public? Who is their ultimate client?

The American Bar Association attempted to meet this issue in ethical consideration 5.18 of its code of professional responsibility, which advises that a corporate lawyer "owes his allegiance to the entity and not to a stockholder, director, officer, employee, representative, or other persons connected with the entity." But as SEC Chairman Harold Williams commented, "While the general thrust of this proposition is certainly correct, it is a statement of very limited utility to the lawyer who, as a practical matter, must deal with the corporation's officers and employees." How is the company lawyer supposed to respond, Williams asked, when management wishes to take a legal risk that the lawyer believes will in the long run adversely affect the corporation as an entity? In fact, Williams wondered how the corporation lawyer can even separate the interests of the entity from the interests of stockholders, directors, officers, and employees, as ethical consideration 5.18 bids him do.[38]

The complications of a lawyer are somewhat greater than those of the accountant by virtue of his special character as a law enforcement officer. Aside from the question of whom he actually represents when his client is as complex as a large corporation, there is his own obligation as a sworn upholder of the judicial system. If he is apprised of past corporate misconduct, he may treat that disclosure as confidential whether his client is the entity or the chief executive officer, but if the misconduct is ongoing then client confidentiality may be inapplicable, especially if criminal activity is involved.

But an issue of this sort cannot be easily separated from the question of the client's identity. If the corporate executive is considered the client, the rule of confidentiality would bind the corporate counsel not to disclose past wrongdoing to others, even to the board of directors; however, the board might reasonably consider itself the corporate client, placing counsel in the predicament of either violating the trust of the executive who had confided his unlawful act or shielding that executive from the client the counsel is presumed to serve.[39] Furthermore, if corporate counsel does take the executive's disclosure to the board he implicates the board simply by providing it with knowledge of wrongdoing; failure on the board's part to act on that knowledge may violate its obligation as trustee for the shareholders, putting counsel in the position of having to consider his legal obligation to them as possible clients.

The role of corporate counsel in advising on compliance with government regulations dealing with occupational health, environmental matters, product safety, and a variety of other areas likewise complicates his life. Violation may be a criminal offense, but compliance may be more costly than a fine and the risk of being caught and found guilty is uncertain. Lloyd Cutler, a Washington lawyer, posed this ethical problem: the lawyer advises his corporate client to comply with the law, but the client decides not to comply or to delay:

> The Code of Professional Responsibility requires us to notify the authorities if our client tells us of his intention to commit a crime. This rule was fashioned to prevent individual crimes of violence. Does it apply to continuing "white collar" crimes, especially a passive crime that consists of failing to correct a condition that has long existed but has only now been made criminally unlawful?[40]

Cutler noted that since such violations can result in injury or death, some would argue that they also are, at least potentially, violent crimes and should be reported. But the effect, according to Cutler, would be to inhibit business firms from seeking legal advice on compliance matters. "We have no definitive answer to this question."[41]

There has been considerable discussion with respect to the relative obligations of inside (employed) counsel and outside (retained) counsel. Some have argued that while in-house attorneys should exercise an independent legal judgment, in difficult situations they might satisfy their responsibility by conferring with outside counsel, whose independence from management can be presumed to be greater. But if a heavier ethical burden is thus placed on outside counsel, the latter should have guaranteed access to the board.[42] On the other hand, Williams observed that "serious questions exist as to whether the ethical responsibilities of someone holding himself out as internal counsel can be any less than those of outside attorneys."[43]

Morris Liebman, senior partner of a Chicago law firm, suggested that the corporation's general counsel is the principal contact between corporate top management and the outside law firm:

> Corporate executives must understand the conflicts and ethical problems now faced by the general counsel. It has become very clear that the general counsel's duties are not just to management. He has other responsibilities to the board and to the shareholder. He may also have other responsibilities to the public interest and to consumers of his corporation's products and services.[44]

The extent to which the corporate lawyer's role has come into question was emphasized by A. A. Sommer, a former SEC commissioner:

> I would suggest that *all* the old verities and truisms about attorneys and their roles are in jeopardy—and unless you are ineradicably dedicated to the preservation of the past that is not all bad. I would suggest that in securities matters, other than those where *advocacy* is clearly proper, the attorney will have to function in a manner more akin to that of the *auditor* than that of the advocate.[45]

From this position it is not a long step to the conclusion that a legal audit is today perhaps a necessary and certainly a desirable accompaniment to the financial audit.[46] At a minimum, "well monitored corporate compliance programs may be the only hope of reducing mounting costs of litigation."[47]

These views with respect to legal monitoring of the corporation, like most views concerning financial audits, are set within the context of the present system of the large corporation conceived as private property and constrained by government regulations. But if a new corporate social strategy is indeed emerging, then the role of the corporate legal monitor would undoubtedly have to expand, like that of the accountant. Well-intentioned corporate initiatives —undertaken in the public interest or in response to national economic and social priorities—cannot be presumed to be free of legal consequences. Even while embracing objectives calculated to enhance the public welfare, the large corporation would have no special license to do as it pleased or to ignore limitations on collective action designed to preserve individual discretion, however much the field for the latter may be shrinking. Collaboration with other corporations and with government itself would presumably be subject to a legal code.

Indeed, evaluation of a corporation's social conduct—a corporate "social profile"—would require some form of legal audit of the impact of the company's actions on society, whether or not this device were simply included in an overall corporate audit that relied on the expertise of a variety of professionals, among them lawyers.

In sum, external evaluation of a corporation's activities, linked to its own internal reporting system, would be necessary for an objective estimation of the company's social impact and contributions. Such a public review might preferably be conducted under private

122

professional auspices as long as these provided sufficient assurance of adequate coverage and independence. The record of a corporation's performance, thus certified, might qualify or disqualify the firm for a leading or preferred role in the loosely designed national economic agenda. Certain professions would thus come into a closer structural relationship with the large corporation, providing a necessary link between it and the relevant government or public agencies.

Notes

1. "The Troubled Professions," *Business Week*, August 16, 1976, p. 127.
2. Mendes Hershman, "Liabilities and Responsibilities of Corporate Officers and Directors," *Business Lawyer* 33 (November 1977):285.
3. *New York Times*, March 4, 1979.
4. "The Troubled Professions," p. 129.
5. Abraham J. Briloff, letter to the editor, *New York Times*, July 12, 1977.
6. Lee J. Seidler, "Auditing and Social Control," in William R. Dill (ed.), *Running the American Corporation* (Englewood Cliffs: Prentice-Hall, 1978), p. 130.
7. Clifford E. Graese, "Accounting, Accountants, and Managers," in Clarence Walton (ed.), *The Ethics of Corporate Conduct* (Englewood Cliffs: Prentice-Hall, 1977), pp. 149–150.
8. Statement by Norman E. Auerbach, *Towards Progress in Professional Accountancy* (White Plains: Coopers & Lybrand, May 1977), p. 3. The hearings were conducted in 1977 by the Subcommittee on Reports, Accounting, and Management of the Committee on Government Operations, U.S. Senate.
9. Seidler, "Auditing and Social Control," p. 120.
10. Geoffrey T. Chalmers, "The Independent Auditor: Guarantor or Guide?" *Business Lawyer* 31 (November 1975):375.
11. Howard F. Stettler, "Two Proposals for Strengthening Auditor Independence," *MSU Business Topics*, (Winter 1980):39.
12. Seidler, "Auditing and Social Control," p. 121.
13. Ibid.
14. Melvin Eisenberg, "Legal Models of Management Structure in the Modern Corporation: Officers, Directors, and Accountants," *California Law Review* 63 (March 1975):417.
15. Ibid., p. 419.
16. Ibid., p. 427.
17. Ibid.
18. Testimony before the Senate Government Operations Subcommittee, reported in the *New York Times*, June 14, 1977.
19. Auerbach, *Towards Progress in Professional Accountancy*, p. 14.
20. *Coopers & Lybrand Newsletter*, November 1977, p. 8.

21. Auerbach, *Towards Progress in Professional Accountancy*, p. 15.
22. Coopers & Lybrand, *Audit Committee Guide*, 2d ed. (White Plains: Coopers & Lybrand, 1976), p. 27.
23. *Wall Street Journal*, February 28, 1979.
24. This account and the quotations come from Hal Lancaster in the *Wall Street Journal*, March 17, 1980.
25. Ibid,
26. Ibid.
27. Ibid.
28. Ibid.
29. Ibid.
30. Eisenberg, "Legal Models," pp. 432–433.
31. Graese, "Accounting, Accountants, and Managers," pp. 157–159.
32. Seidler, "Auditing and Social Control," p. 133.
33. Eisenberg, "Legal Models," p. 417.
34. *Business Week*, June 6, 1977, pp. 84–86, reported on a number of such recommendations. One of the more detailed prescriptions has been made by John C. Burton, former chief accountant of the SEC, in "The Profession's Institutional Structure in the 1980s," *Journal of Accountancy* 145 (April 1978):63–69.
35. Eisenberg, "Legal Models," pp. 436–437. Eisenberg's fidelity to the underlying system of relations is explicit in his *Structure of the Corporation* (Boston: Little, Brown, 1976), p. 319.
36. American Institute of Certified Public Accountants, *The Measurement of Corporate Social Performance* (New York: AICPA, 1977), pp. 255–257, 262.
37. "The GAO's Long Reach Comes under Fire," *Business Week*, July 9, 1979, pp. 62–63.
38. Harold M. Williams, "Corporate Accountability and the Lawyer's Role," *Business Lawyer* 34 (November 1978):12.
39. Geoffrey Hazard, "Talking to Your Lawyer: The Ethics of the Corporate-Legal Relationship," *MBA*, May 1978, pp. 20–21.
40. Lloyd N. Cutler, "The Development of New Specialties: OSHA, ERISA, and the Relationship with Government," *Business Lawyer* 34 (February 1979):941.
41. Ibid.
42. Ronald D. Rotunda, "Law, Lawyers, and Managers," in Walton (ed.), *The Ethics of Corporate Conduct*, pp. 135–136.
43. Williams, "Corporate Accountability," p. 15.
44. Morris I. Liebman, "The Change in Client Relationships: The Interface with General Counsel," *Business Lawyer* 34 (February 1979):958.
45. Francis M. Wheat, "The Impact of SEC Professional Responsibility Standards," *Business Lawyer* 34 (February 1979):970.
46. "Can Accountants Uncover Management Fraud?" *Business Week*, July 10, 1978, p. 92; see also Christopher Stone, *Where the Law Ends*, (New York: Harper & Row, 1975), p. 42.
47. John P. Austin, "The Shift to Litigation," *Business Lawyer* 34 (February 1979):935.

8

Federal Chartering of National Corporations

The U.S. federal system has preserved the principle that a corporation is the grant of a franchise by a sovereign state. Beginning in Massachusetts in 1811 and becoming standard practice in all states by 1875, such grants were made under general incorporation laws rather than through negotiated agreements between petitioning incorporators and state legislatures. With the growth in size of corporations and the emergence by the end of the nineteenth century of the large, modern corporation, the coordination of national production, marketing, and financial functions called for firmer organizational control: "As early as 1865 we find the germ of the modern conception of corporate power—the belief that the rights of the participants as well as the technical conduct of the business must be subject to managerial discretion."[1]

Since the federal system permitted a company to incorporate in one state and to operate in all states, states competed for the incorporation business. The benefits came not only as revenue to the state itself for the grant of the charter but also as income to the whole legal and judicial fraternity of the state for services in connection with legal matters arising under the charter. Given the pressure for greater management control of the expanding firm, state competition over corporate chartering resulted in reduced restrictions, affirmatively "granting to corporate management the most extreme powers not only to operate the business but also to alter or take away pre-existing rights of stockholders."[2]

State regulation of corporate conduct followed the same pattern. Early efforts at social legislation, particularly in the field of employment and working conditions, were undercut not only by the U.S. Supreme Court's interpretation of private property and the rights of contract but also by state legislative concern that corporations would simply take their business elsewhere: "There is only a limited area in which states can vary the quality and quantity of regulation of internal corporate affairs without inducing those corporations to shun the state."[3]

The result has been a virtual abdication by states of efforts at controlling corporate conduct. Incorporation procedures "are almost necessarily limited to more and more refined forms of enabling legislation," heavily weighted in favor of management. "The watchwords of recent statutory revisions— 'flexibility,' 'modernization,' 'streamlining' and like terms—mask the reality: that state corporation laws are strongly, usually overwhelmingly, pro-management and anti-shareholder, because they affirmatively resolve almost all key issues in favor of the former and against the latter."[4]

Delaware has achieved the dubious but highly prized distinction of leading in the "race to the bottom." Its corporation law gives greater freedom to pay dividends and distribute assets; greater ease of amending the corporate charter; less restriction on mortgaging, leasing, and merging assets; clearer rights of indemnification of directors and officers for fines assessed; and fewer preemptive rights to shareholders. The Delaware courts have interpreted the law, with few exceptions, in ways favorable to management.[5] It is scarcely surprising that approximately half the corporations listed on the New York Stock Exchange have found it advantageous to incorporate in Delaware; other states, however, have not abandoned the competition for corporate favor: "The existing processes are not structured to produce, nor could they be restructured to yield, a different sort of corporation law on the state level."[6]

The placement of incorporation powers in the states and their inability to initiate legislative protection of parties affected by the actions of corporations have prompted Congress to pass laws dealing with the actions of corporations but not with the corporations themselves, with policy rather than structure. Insofar as any structural requirements have been imposed, they have been under cover of specialized protection of investor interests, disregarding the role of the big national corporation in society at large. From time to time the federal courts have nudged the SEC in the direction of defining investor interests more broadly, as I noted in previous chapters, but the investor still remains the hinge on which must swing the door of federal intervention in corporate structure. As a former chairman of the SEC, William Cary, remarked wryly: "It seems anomalous to jigsaw every kind of corporate dispute into the federal courts through the securities acts as they are presently written."[7] To Cary, as to a number of other observers, the present federal abdication to the states of responsibility for standards of incorporation is unfortunate. He asked

> whether the policy of a single state should be permitted to grant management unilateral control untrammeled by other interests. Should one state set social policy in the corporate field when a cornerstone of that policy is to stay ahead of (or behind) the rest? . . . There is a need for uniformity in standards to prevent the application of Gresham's law.[8]

Federal Minimum Standards

The indictment of states as inevitably lax in prescribing standards of corporate responsibility has elicited proposals for federal incorporation. Cary, with memories of Washington political infighting vivid in his mind, suggested an intermediate alternative. The chartering of business firms would be left to the states, but the federal government would fix minimum standards. His proposal rested not on an academic ideal but on what he argued is a realistic possibility. Federal incorporation would arouse too strong an opposition from business to stand any chance of winning congressional approval, short of "catastrophic depression or a corporate debacle." "National corporations" sounds too close to "nationalization," too convenient a vehicle for government control, to be politically acceptable. Hence the move to a more realistic second best: the federal government should prescribe minimum corporation law provisions for companies engaged in interstate commerce; such provisions would be construed by the federal courts.[9]

Cary's major uniform provisions included fiduciary standards with respect to directors and officers; limitations on managerial authority to amend bylaws, initiate actions, and draw up the agenda for shareholder meetings; shareholder authorization for certain kinds of transactions; abolition of nonvoting shares; limits on indemnification of directors; and protection of shareholders from intracorporate actions designed to benefit management or directors. Perhaps, Cary conceded, an inquiry should be opened to reconsider the whole question of governance of the corporation, including its relation to the public, but that is something for the future. In the meantime, "the first step is to escape from the present predicament," wherein one state can jeopardize in its own behalf the nation's interest in maintaining standards of corporate responsibility.[10]

Ernest Folk, who served as chief staff aide to the 1967 Delaware Corporation Law Revision Commission, reached substantially the same position as Cary. That commission concluded:

> It is clear that the major protections to investors, creditors, employees, customers, and the general public have come, and must continue to come, from Federal legislation and not from state corporation acts. . . . Any attempt to provide such regulations in the public interest through state incorporation acts and similar legislation would only drive corporations out of the state to more hospitable jurisdictions.[11]

Speaking for himself, Folk argued that to expect states to regulate corporate conduct "is to indulge in an illusion." Corporation laws at the state level can be of the enabling variety only, creating but not effectively controlling corporations. Raising standards of corporate responsibility requires federal legislation. Nevertheless, Folk favored leaving the states to devise their own corporate forms. He would, however, "chasten" state corporation laws by superimposing on them federal legislative standards of managerial responsibility for corporations in interstate commerce: "Such a statute should supplement existing state statute and case law. It should replace existing state law only to the extent that the presumably higher federal standards of managerial responsibility should override inconsistent state law." Folk believed that the result would be to turn back the movement in the states, "now far advanced, towards total management discretion."[12]

Federal Incorporation

Cary premised his case for retaining the system of state incorporation, while formulating federal minimum standards, on the political improbability of getting anything more. He pointed out that proposals for federal incorporation have been raised repeatedly in Congress and repeatedly have been squelched. But what to Cary signaled hopelessness has suggested to others—notably Ralph Nader and Donald Schwartz—that the idea cannot be downed. Nader and Schwartz observed that agitation for federal incorporation goes back at least a hundred years, has been endorsed by prominent political figures (President Theodore Roosevelt, in a 1905 message to Congress, among others), and has been bought off by a variety of regulatory reforms but still keeps returning to the congressional agenda.[13] In similar vein, Phillip Blumberg concluded that "the increasing abdication by the various states of control over the internal conduct of corporate affairs and the increased concern with the role of the large corporation in society make enactment of a federal incorporation statute within the next 15 years a realistic possibility."[14]

In short, this camp believes that the case for federal incorporation should be considered on its merits: "There will be time enough for political practicalities to become part of the process."[15]

As for the merits, proponents of federal chartering argue that minimum standards would not meet the issue. Whatever standards Congress might impose could not possibly cover all potential areas of management discretion. Within whatever discretionary space were left to the states, states would continue to compete with each other by offering management more leeway: "Law-makers at the state level will continue to pull one way toward corporate management while law-makers at the federal level tug the other way, toward a balanced national corporate policy. Even if federal corporate standards were drafted with extraordinary care and skill, they would be subject to this conflict."[16]

Beyond the question of political feasibility lies a different sense of urgency and purpose between the two camps of reformers. Corporate reform can be considered from opposite perspectives: one concentrates on protecting the interests of the corporation's shareholders; the other is concerned also with the interests of the public. Whereas the first seeks to constrain the powers of management in dealing with shareholder interests, the second seeks to constrain the powers of the corporation as an institution in dealing with the public. By and large, the minimum standards approach conforms to the first point of view; the federal incorporation approach is more concerned with the second. Thus Schwartz, commenting on Cary: "The chief defect of his program is its failure to deal with . . . the adverse impact of corporate power on society."[17] The minimum standards approach would sweep in all corporations operating in interstate commerce—a very considerable number. Cary suggested a line be drawn arbitrarily to exclude companies with assets under $250,000 and fewer than fifty shareholders. Advocates of federal incorporation generally are satisfied with covering the largest firms. Nader suggested the seven hundred largest; Schwartz would include the largest one thousand.

The federal chartering proposals have differed in some respects. In summary, Schwartz would

> declare that a purpose of the corporation is to advance the non-stockholder interests affected by the corporation
>
> require extensive disclosure of a broad range of corporate matters relating to both shareholder and public interests
>
> facilitate private interdiction of corporate wrongs that adversely affect either stockholder or nonstockholder interests and provide the latter with standing in court by the broader declaration of corporate purpose
>
> provide liberalized methods of nominating and electing directors
>
> alter the procedures of the board of directors, such as limiting board size in order to promote a better working environment; limiting the number of directorships any one individual may hold; requiring appointment of an audit committee and a public policy committee, both of which would issue reports on their activities; requiring a majority of directors to be outsiders; giving serious consideration to placing a cadre of professional directors on the board and to providing outside directors with staff
>
> change some rules regarding liability of directors in respect to the management of the corporation
>
> restrict management's ability to protect its own discretion
>
> broaden stockholders' protection against management over-reaching.[18]

Nader's proposal covered much of the same territory but went further. With respect to internal government of the corporation, he would provide for a full-time board, with a majority of outside directors. Nader would also require more extensive public disclosure of company effects on the environment, of employment practices, of the basis for advertising claims, of lobbying activities, and of ties with other companies. This information would be compiled in a corporate register published by the federal government. Community impact statements would have to be prepared when a company wished to relocate a plant. In relations with employees, a company would have to comply with an employee bill of rights protecting workers who criticized company practices, giving them a right to inspect their personnel files, and prohibiting penalties on workers who refused to follow orders inconsistent with their consciences or threatening to their health and safety. Finally, corporate acquisitions within the circle of large corporations would be strictly controlled.[19]

Curiously, Schwartz and Nader took a basically conservative stance toward modifying the structure of the large corporation. Both left the shareholders as the basic constituency, even while admitting that others—and the public at large—have clear interests in corporate dealings. Shareholders elect directors; directors select management; a majority of directors must be outsiders, but the idea of public or professional directors was deferred to future consideration. In essence, both would preserve the large corporation as private property (even though vested with public interest) governed by an economic motivation (even though social concerns would be taken into account). Both proposals sought to protect the effective operation of the market by guarding against politicization of the corporation from inside (though Nader asked that a particular director be assigned the responsibility of looking after the welfare of a specialized interest such as consumers or dealers, and both favored giving special and public groups a clearer standing in court when their interests were affected). Finally, Schwartz and Nader also would strengthen the market discipline of the corporation (though Schwartz considered specific legislative provisions concerning mergers and market shares too complex and divisive a matter to include within a general chartering law).

Schwartz was perhaps most explicit in this defense of shareholders' property rights in a competitive market:

> While corporations do resemble political bodies, as measured by their impact, reform that would conform their structure to that of political bodies might destroy the ability of corporations to func-

tion as economic units. . . . The composition of the board along political lines would cause resource allocation decisions to be made politically rather than by market considerations since some of the decision makers would have no economic concern for the enterprise. The main issue here is whether economic disciplines or central economic planning should be the mechanism by which we decide economic issues. . . .

We must try to improve the system we know until we can identify a better one. Politicalization of the corporation is not a better system in my opinion because it will aggravate the problems of the corporation without effectively dealing with the social problems. But we ought not delude ourselves into thinking that the marketplace is doing a better job than the facts justify since that will only lull us into false complacency.[20]

So, while allowing stockholders to "enjoy the practical fulfillment of their role" and strengthening the "stockholder democracy process within the corporation," some means must also be devised "to increase managerial sensitivity to outside interests." Schwartz would attempt to do this by promoting fuller disclosure, encouraging a concern among both corporations and regulatory agencies for the externalities of economic operations, and giving injured parties easier access to the courts.[21]

Schwartz seemed unwilling to recognize that the essentially conservative nature of this position ("In large part, this is a codification of much of the recent writing about the corporation") stood at odds with his professed purpose. In referring to his proposed "federal chartering act," he recommended that it contain a "statement of the purpose and the nature of the large corporation—that it is not wholly or solely concerned with maximizing profits":

The law might specify that the interests and concerns of the corporation embrace not only those of the stockholders, but also those of the larger community directly affected by the corporation's activities, including employees and consumers and those who might be styled the "neighbors" of the corporation. Accordingly, management is expected, or at least privileged, to balance the interests of owners with the interests of other community interests.[22]

But to leave with management—whether or not elected by outside directors responsive to a newly resurgent body of shareholders—the discretion as to how the interests of the latter are to be balanced against the interests of all others is *necessarily* to leave to management a political decision if that discretion is actually exercised. But

Schwartz disavowed the politicized corporate decision and rested his preference with economic disciplines. On the other hand, if management in fact followed the economic disciplines, it would have to disregard (except to the present very limited degree) the larger public interests that Schwartz would have corporations embrace and the neglect of which he called the chief defect of Cary's minimum standards approach.

There seems to be an unwillingness on the part of many advocates of federal chartering to recognize that without significant structural change in the corporation itself, most of the objectives they seek could as readily be realized by regulatory legislation without federal chartering. Such advocates do indeed appreciate that "some restructuring of the corporation is needed,"[23] but for the most part they have in mind measures to strengthen the position of shareholders against management. The fundamental issue, which is unavoidable if public interest in large-scale corporate activity is asserted with any vigor, goes to the concept of the big corporation as private property embodying private discretion in its use, except insofar as specifically restrained by government regulation. Once that point is clear, any movement to modify the present status of the large corporation would necessarily involve more basic structural changes than the proponents of federal chartering seem to recognize, which raises the question of whether federal incorporation has any purpose at all if limited to the issues of what political body grants the charter and what federal restrictions (basically, regulatory measures of the familiar type) should obtain.

Is Federal Chartering Relevant?

Whether federal chartering makes sense depends entirely on the reasons for invoking this device. To those who see it as an instrument permitting the federal government to regulate corporations more effectively, it may well be, as Christopher Stone said, "a superfluous, intervening step."[24] The federal government can regulate without chartering. This objection would probably apply equally to minor structural changes, such as requiring that a majority of directors be outsiders or that the board appoint an audit committee. Such changes can be instituted by appropriate construction of existing securities legislation.

If the intent is more basic structural modification, then the grounds for federal incorporation are clearer. Even if such changes were to be introduced piecemeal, the new institutional edifice could be more easily assembled under a single jurisdiction. Provision for public directors, the gradual development of a corporate social audit characterized by a significant degree of standardization (applied general principles), the monitoring of corporate performance by approved professional standards, a preferred part in national priority programs on the basis of a corporation's certified economic and social performance—these and other possible structural ingredients of a new national policy for large corporations would seem to be better served by combining them in a corporate charter than by imposing a regulatory framework on top of state charters. The result might not in fact be much different—the same destination might be reached by either road—but at least the federal route would sweep away the anachronism of state incorporation of national corporations larger, and with broader jurisdictions, than the chartering entity itself.

Federal chartering could be made mandatory for corporations above a certain size. State charters conforming to minimum federal standards would still be available to smaller companies, though these should have the option of federal incorporation, which would carry benefits such as the opportunity to participate on preferable terms in programs given social precedence.

It is hard to avoid the conclusion—Cary's conclusion—that the chief resistance to federal incorporation rests on the fear that it portends greater government intervention in the "private" corporation. A state charter distances the corporation from Washington, at least symbolically, but only symbolically. If indeed the large corporation is being pressured into seeking a new social strategy for itself, that strategy must relate to the nation at large. A federal charter may then become symbolic, and possibly only symbolic, of the new corporate structure that facilitates the new strategy. But symbols are important in reinforcing attitudes: the national status of large corporations may not be so much an idea whose time has come as a reality in need of formal recognition.

Notes

1. A. A. Berle, Jr., and Gardiner C. Means, "Corporation," *Encyclopedia of Social Sciences* (New York: Macmillan, 1937), vol. 4, p. 417.
2. Ibid., p. 418.

3. E. L. Folk III, "State Statutes: Their Role in Prescribing Norms of Responsible Management Conduct," *Business Lawyer* 31 (February 1976):1034.
4. Ibid., pp. 1051, 1052.
5. William L. Cary examined the Delaware situation in detail in "Federalism and Corporate Law: Reflections upon Delaware," *Yale Law Journal* 83 (March 1974):663–705.
6. Folk, "State Statutes," p. 1058.
7. Cary, "Federalism and Corporate Law," p. 700.
8. Ibid., p. 698.
9. Idem.
10. Ibid., pp. 700–701.
11. Ibid., p. 666.
12. Folk, "State Statutes," pp. 1074, 1080.
13. Ralph Nader, "The Case for Federal Chartering," in Ralph Nader and Mark Green (eds.), *Corporate Power in America* (New York: Grossman, 1973); Ralph Nader, Mark Green, and Joel Seligman, *Constitutionalizing the Corporation: The Case for Chartering of Giant Corporations* (Washington, D.C.: Corporate Accountability Research Group, 1976); Donald E. Schwartz, "A Case for Federal Chartering of Corporations," *Business Lawyer* 31 (February 1976):1126–1127.
14. Phillip I. Blumberg, "Reflections on Proposals for Corporate Reform through Change in the Composition of the Board of Directors: 'Special Interest' or 'Public' Directors," *Boston University Law Review* 53 (May 1973):572.
15. Schwartz, "A Case for Federal Chartering," p. 1139.
16. Joel F. Henning, "Federal Corporate Chartering for Big Business: An Idea Whose Time Has Come," *DePaul Law Review* 21 (1972, Part II, Symposium on Federal–State Relations):915.
17. Schwartz, "A Case for Federal Chartering," p. 1140.
18. Ibid., passim.
19. Nader, "The Case for Federal Chartering," passim.
20. Schwartz, "A Case for Federal Chartering," pp. 1143–1144.
21. Ibid., p. 1145.
22. Ibid., p. 1148.
23. Ibid., p. 1144.
24. "A Step Toward the Federal Corporate Charter," *Business Week*, June 21, 1976, p. 84.

9

Foreign Operations of U.S. Corporations

If large corporations affect their society in ways that generate public and political pressures to channel that impact (at first defensively then, potentially, constructively), the same can be said of corporate foreign operations. Foreign pressures can be brought to bear directly on the company (by insurgent workers, politicians, or reform governments, for example), but pressures may also be transmitted through the U.S. government: the foreign government speaks to Washington and the U.S. government deals with the company. In either event, the corporation's overseas operations involve public policy.

The Business of America Abroad

In an earlier day, governed by the principle if not the practice of a free private market, a company's foreign operations, like its domestic business, were considered its own affair—its accepted risk, its seized opportunity. Private fortunes were made and sometimes lost in overseas trading, and aside from occasional governmental interventions to preserve "freedom of the seas" and an "open door," free trade prevailed. American society benefited from U.S. companies' foreign economic activities just as from their domestic activities—both contributed to growth and prosperity—but this result was presumed to flow from private initiative and not government action.

Even with the twentieth-century growth of U.S. multinational corporations, this traditional view continued. As Robert Gilpin observed: "Corporate expansionism is largely divorced from the larger arena of world politics. The multinational corporation is regarded as an independent actor on the international scene. The relationship between American corporations and the United States government is held to be an 'arm's length' one."[1]

Today this simplistic view is crumbling. The radical conception of the large American corporation as an exploiter of foreign labor and resources gained currency in the developing countries following World War II. The view that American big business (and that of other western powers) constituted an agent of economic imperialism became a major theme in the independence movements that spread rapidly through the Third World, even in countries (notably in Latin America) that for years had been formally independent but saw themselves as dependents of the industrialized nations, particularly the United States. The fact of their political independence seemed to provide little protection against the overweening economic power of the large multinational corporations, which could set their own terms on a take it or leave it basis, confident that if one developing country (or politician) refused to play ball another would be only too eager to join the game. In this period, the 1950s and early 1960s, American multinationals seemed to dominate the international economy; some analysts asserted that the nation-state was incapable of countering the more mobile organization and wealth of a worldwide corporation. Sovereignty was held at bay: "The long-run trend will be toward the dwindling of the power of the national state relative to the corporation."[2] Observers most convinced of this development foresaw a future in which a limited number of multinational corporations, beholden to no country, would control the international economy.

This widespread ascription of power to the giant, world-ranging corporation aroused resentment in the developing countries. Neocolonialism, with the multinationals its instrument, led them to seek constraining codes of conduct through a United Nations Commission on Transnational Corporations. The intricate web of operations in which a large multinational was engaged—obtaining resources here, processing them there, assembling goods in still other locations, marketing finished products elsewhere—suggested a sinister means of disguising profits, avoiding taxes, and increasing leverage in dealing with any single country. Hence the U.N. commission's recommendation for greater disclosure of information in such areas as employment and production practices, transfer pricing, new investments, research activities and product development, proposed mergers, marketing policies, and pollution effects.

The Third World sense of exploitation inevitably became a political issue involving the U.S. government. The relation was made explicit by congressional passage of the Foreign Corrupt Practices Act in 1977, after discovery of innumerable cases of U.S. businesses' bribing foreign officials to obtain contracts. It was no use to say that such corruption required two parties, one from the complaining country. The spotlight rested on the big company with the wealth to beguile local accomplices. The U.S. Congress in effect admitted as much.

The public policy issues raised by the activities of freewheeling multinational corporations came home to the United States in an even more direct way. At times the relation between business and government has been revealed as collaborationist in the covert formulation of foreign policy. There is no need to rehash the unsavory details of ITT-CIA negotiations with respect to besmirching and undermining the Allende regime in Chile. Hearings before the Senate Foreign Relations Committee in 1976 suggested on another front a complex interaction between major U.S. weapons manufacturers and the U.S. Department of Defense. The president of Grumman, for example, testified that his company had been encouraged by military officials to solicit orders from Iran for the sophisticated F-14 fighter even though clearance for the plane's sale to a foreign government had not been authorized: "Once the Shah became interested, great pressure then developed on the Administration to make the plane available to satisfy the Iranian Government," Senator Frank Church charged.[3] This single instance—which presumably was more typical than not of the private-public partnership in arms merchandising—acquired special significance in light of the subsequent turbulent overthrow of the shah and the violent anti-American sentiment aroused by his efforts at turning Iran, with American assistance, into a Middle Eastern military power. Clearly this episode involved more than simple free market economics on the part of an American company.

An even more fundamental connection between American corporate operations overseas and U.S. political objectives was analyzed by Robert Gilpin, professor of political science and international affairs at Princeton University. In brief, the surge of direct American foreign investment after World War II displaced the British financial houses as the "principal mechanism for integrating the non-Communist world economy":

> Although government officials did not foresee that American corporations would expand so as to establish a significant American presence in and impact on all the economies of the non-Communist world, American policies did encourage and protect corporate expansionism after World War II. American tax policy, the insistence that American subsidiaries in the Common Market be treated as "European" corporations, and much later, the creation of the Overseas Private Investment Corporation (1969) to insure foreign investments are but three examples of measures designed to foster corporate expansionism.[4]

Gilpin explicitly recognized that the American government had little or no intention of drafting a grand design based on corporate expansion abroad. Rather, there came a gradual realization "that the growing overseas empires of American corporations could be made to serve the larger interests of the United States"—sometimes, perhaps frequently, even against the wishes of the corporations themselves. He singled out, from among many possible examples of this interplay, the matter of dealing with the American balance of payments:

> By the late 1950s, the payments drain of overseas military, diplomatic, and foreign aid commitments had caused a serious balance of payments deficit for the United States. As this deficit became more serious, the multinational corporations and their rapidly growing foreign earnings were recognized as major national assets which could help finance America's global hegemonic position.
>
> In conjunction with the international position of the dollar and with nuclear supremacy, the multinational corporation became one of the three cornerstones of American hegemony. These three elements of American power interacted with and reinforced one another. . . . American political and military supremacy arising out of World War II was a necessary precondition for the predominant position of American multinational corporations in the

139

world economy. But the reciprocal of this is also true: corporate expansionism in turn became a support of America's international political and military position.[5]

The underlying complementary sharing of interests—even if not always harmonious and certainly not very systematic—belied both the traditional conception of the American corporation as a free agent in a free market and the Marxist view of the U.S. company as a tool of imperialism. Instead, "the corporations and the United States government have tended to share an overlapping and complementary set of interests. . . . American hegemony in the contemporary world has rested, in part, on the vast international operations of American corporations."[6] The corporations would themselves have preferred to loosen the ties to the home government, operating solely in their own interests, neutral toward the world at large, stateless entities (or, in periods of extreme hubris, statelike entities). But in the final analysis (and in the frequent preliminary reckonings) no corporation, however large or wealthy, could field an army or threaten sanctions stronger than severance of relations.

The multinational corporations have recognized their limitations even if they have used their own importance to the nation in bargaining for policies suited to their own advantage. The chairman of Dow Chemical, a leader among the multinationals, put the matter succinctly: "By the United States law an American corporation operating in another nation is obliged to conform to the dictates of the Federal Government, executive, legislative and judicial. It is thus, through no choice of its own, to some extent an instrument of American policy."[7] And a former assistant secretary of commerce observed: "For the enterprise not to be under control of the U.S. government would mean that the government had abdicated a series of important economic decisions to the boardrooms of these companies."[8]

For this variety of reasons, then, the foreign operations of American corporations become entangled with public policy. They influence society—the foreign societies in which they function in the first instance and then American society. Their operations therefore cannot be viewed as public only insofar as they encourage economic growth and prosperity; in both overseas and domestic functioning the big corporations can no longer be considered as simply the private property of shareholders and free to exercise discretion within regulatory limits. These businesses already affect public interests too deeply, both adversely and favorably, and possess too great a potential for advancing national interests affirmatively to be dealt with by government casually: "The current absence of U.S. policy towards the multinationals is a dereliction of duty."[9]

Interdependence versus Nationalism

The remarkable economic growth of the western industrialized nations in the period after World War II rested largely on a resurgence of relatively free international trade. Of course there were always limits on such freedom—protective gambits used in varying degree, whether tariffs, quotas, government home purchase policies, or product specifications—but despite these measures the thrust of international economic relations tended toward liberalization. Thus, successive rounds of the General Agreement on Tariffs and Trade sought to lessen restrictions; likewise, the European Economic Community and its associated countries created an enormous new free-trading area from which outsiders could benefit by the simple device of domiciling a subsidiary in one of the member countries.

The underlying principle of free international trade is comparative advantage: each country specializes in those types of production in which it is most cost efficient. Comparative advantage thus translates as competitive advantage, and for a country to retain its lead in any product field it must stay ahead of other producers by improving the product or the production process, by keeping labor costs in a satisfactory relation to productivity, or by obtaining cheaper raw materials. In all these respects except the last the western powers had a significant lead over the rest of the world in the early years after World War II. Then the tide began to turn, slowly at first. By the late 1960s Japan—hardly an underdeveloped country—was recognized as a serious competitor in an ever increasing number of fields that the West had once dominated. Behind Japan loomed a file of developing nations building up a comparative advantage, resting largely on low labor costs, in a number of basic industries such as textiles, steel, and shipbuilding. The list kept growing.

Even in these relatively uncomplicated fields the mass production techniques necessary for world trade would not have been forthcoming without the intrusion of the western multinationals.

141

Taking advantage of low wages and disciplined labor, they invested abroad in mills and plants not so much to produce for the local market as to produce for export. Sometimes the completed product, sometimes a component, was exported back to the home market for sale or final processing. Comparative advantage was moving away from the western countries in a small but increasing number of industries.

The shift in competitive advantage was accelerated as the multinationals began setting up overseas operations employing both routine technologies and more advanced types of production. The newer technologies frequently did not require any more advanced skills, and the developing nations had an ample supply of easily trained, compliant, and inexpensive labor. Protectionist sentiment began to surge in western societies, particularly after the recession of 1974-1975. But now western governments faced a dilemma. Their postwar prosperity had depended on a free competitive market, based on comparative advantage and implying specialization. Specialization, in turn, implies interdependence. In order to concentrate on activities at which it excels, one country gives up doing what other countries can do better. To remain steadfast to the free trade principle thus required that the industrialized countries abandon to the developing nations those lines of production in which the latter could now perform more effectively; the industrialized countries would then move on to more sophisticated kinds of technology and products, notably those associated with advanced chemistry, electronics, computers, and, more recently, biotechnology. The alternative would be to give up on free trade and international interdependence, reverting to mercantilism and nationalism, which would mean foregoing cheaper consumption and greater product variety. The prospect sounded like a backward step, but to adhere to the free-trade philosophy had drawbacks, too. Industries that had been large-scale employers, finding themselves unable to compete with low-cost imports, would have to close down, laying off workers. Expensive assets would sit idle and unemployed workers would be compensated for producing nothing. A country would draw down its balance of payments by importing goods it could have produced at home, though not as cheaply as the countries from which they were now imported could produce them.

The stock answer to such observations has been that this is the way the free competitive system is supposed to work. Motivating management and workers to transfer their capabilities to new lines of activity not yet pursued or vigorously exploited elsewhere and abandoning former activities to recently industrializing countries would leave everyone better off. Economic incentive would move both developed and developing economies onto higher planes of productivity. Comparative advantage and specialization would play their roles; new relationships of interdependence would be established to worldwide benefit. Who wished to return to the insularity of nationalism?

This argument, repeated daily in the public press and official statements, has met with increasing resistance. The shift from one type of production to another requires not only new technical developments but often years of experimentation and experience as well. The new processes do not require the same numbers of people (let alone the same people—a different generation is usually involved). In the meantime the unemployed become functionless. Communities are sometimes left to stagnate. Countries foresake basic fields of production—even domestic food production—in search of items they can make and sell more cheaply than competitors can.

The vise effect of international competition has been masked under the euphemism of interdependence, a word intended to connote a drawing together of people within a world community. But the interdependence based on comparative advantage is not so much a drawing together on a field of common interest as a drawing apart on a field of fierce economic competition in which livelihoods and lifestyles are at stake. Interdependence necessarily exists in a world where resources are distributed unevenly, but interdependence can take other forms than a race to see who can produce something most cheaply regardless of the conditions under which the goods are made. A society can be interdependent with other nations in ways that it chooses for itself and for purposes it determines for itself even though compromises are necessary precisely because mutual dependence is involved. Interdependence is not an inevitable economic mold clamped down (by whom?) on all peoples.

In the same way that the limited economic concept of interdependence has acquired a false luster, an equally limited concept of nationalism has been given a bad repute. Nationalism tends to be associated with either isolation or imperialism—both bad. But nationalism can also mean regard for the preservation of a people's

143

own sense of social coherence, of a sense of identity as well as community, of balance between economic pursuits and culture—more attractive values than the implementation of a world assembly line.

"It does not now seem obvious," wrote Keynes in a remarkable essay published in 1933, "that a great concentration of national effort on the capture of foreign trade, that the penetration of a country's economic structure by the resources and the influence of foreign capitalists, and that a close dependence of our own economic life on the fluctuating economic policies of foreign countries are safeguards and assurances of international peace."[10] The motive of economic advantage in trade seemed questionable to Keynes, who recognized the remoteness of interest between those whose advantage was in fact being assured and those who were affected by the former's operations:

> I sympathize therefore with those who would minimize rather than with those who would maximize economic entanglements among nations. Ideas, knowledge, science, hospitality, travel— these are the things which should of their nature be international. But let goods be homespun wherever it is reasonably and conveniently possible, and, above all, let finance be primarily national.[11]

Keynes saw the problem as the balance between economic and noneconomic forces. He was quite prepared to admit that a "considerable degree of international specialization is necessary . . . dictated by wide differences of climate, natural resources, native aptitudes, level of culture and density of population." Nevertheless, he had come to believe that over an "increasingly wide range of industrial products, and perhaps of agricultural products also," the advantage of bringing the product and the consumer together within the same social organization was greater than economy bought at the price of greater national dependence on others: "A moderate increase in the real cost of primary and manufactured products consequent on greater self-sufficiency may cease to be of serious consequence when weighed in the balance against advantages of a different kind."[12] However, self-sufficiency was no more to be pursued as a dogma than was comparative advantage; the former represented a flexible policy designed to achieve a society richer in more ways than simply the material:

> We do not wish, therefore, to be at the mercy of world forces working out, or trying to work out, some uniform equilibrium ac-

cording to the ideal principles, if they can be called such, of *laissez-faire* capitalism. . . . We wish to be our own masters. . . .

Thus, regarded from this point of view, the policy of increased self-sufficiency is to be considered, not as an ideal in itself, but as directed to the creation of an environment in which other ideals can be safely and conveniently pursued.[13]

From this perspective the issue of what economic relations are to be pursued by a society is a political question to be resolved by a political process of discussion and compromise, a question involving the definition of objectives and the ranking of social priorities, just as with respect to domestic economic and social policy.

International Economic Policy and the Corporation

Once the belief is laid aside that a free international market is controlling of domestic economics, a number of public policy issues are up for debate. Understandably, some involve lines of thinking that are heresy by traditional standards; for example, whether direct overseas investment is preferable to domestic investment may not be a matter for corporations to decide on their own. Even if a higher rate of profit might be earned by the company, the consequence might be to diminish the development of the domestic economy.

This is a sensitive issue. For one thing, it challenges the discretion of corporate management, raising all the concerns relating to the rights of private property that were reviewed earlier. In addition, the question of corporate sovereignty generates an inconclusive debate between those who argue that direct foreign investment deprives workers at home of jobs they might otherwise have had and those who argue that those jobs would have been lost anyway to cheaper foreign competition. Some observers contend that the retention, through direct investment abroad, of markets that otherwise would have been lost to foreign competitors permits at least a continuing flow of domestically produced components; insures a return flow of profits that can be invested at home; and may increase the demand for other home produced exports. But what if the subsidiaries abroad begin exporting to additional markets formerly served by domestic producers? And the subsidiaries abroad no longer need to rely on components from the country of origin? And the profits earned abroad are more profitably invested abroad?

145

From a western point of view, the principles of free trade were best defended when technology changed more slowly and when the world was organized into a two-tier system of industrialized and nonindustrialized nations so that comparative advantage for the latter meant cheap production of raw materials for the former. The situation today is different, and imports from industrializing countries displace domestic goods in the industrialized nations at an accelerating rate. The free market threatens the home market. Edmund Dell, former British secretary for trade, himself disposed to champion as free a trade as possible, nevertheless commented:

> Government has been dragged back to face the fact that in order to discharge its responsibilities it must have a capacity to intervene, that it cannot exclude itself on principle from the possibility of action. . . . It is an odd economic conception that of all the forces that may operate in a market, governments alone must be prohibited from taking direct action to strengthen their nation's economic and industrial structure, however powerful their conviction that they can act usefully in that sense.[14]

Despite their predilection for supporting the free trade system on which western prosperity has depended, governments, business managements, and labor unions gingerly have recognized the need for some form of industrial policy that seeks to manage the transition to a sustainable and desirable industrial structure. The aim is to prevent the obsolescence of both workers and assets. One objective might indeed be to stimulate innovation; another, systematically to upgrade products and production methods in an industry as new technology appears, thereby precluding the sudden invasion of foreign competitors. In still other cases, the objective might be to reorganize an industry in the most economically efficient way possible, with attention to social as well as economic circumstances. Even if less efficient than a foreign competitor, the new domestic structure would provide people with a sense of social purpose that could not be gained from idleness and unemployment compensation; in the meantime alternatives could be explored.

John Pinder, director of the Policy Studies Institute of London, made this case forcefully:

> A combination of quick changes and slow adjustments has disrupted many sectors of manufacturing which are the backbone of our industrial economies and their international trade. The changes are rapid not only because of the pace of technological

146

development, but also because of the shrinking of an international economy in which there are so many different levels, rates of growth and economic types. With the irruption of imports from low-wage countries such as Hong-Kong or high-growth countries such as Japan, industrial sectors in Europe and North America, as diverse as textiles, clothing, footwear, radio and television, steel, shipbuilding and passenger cars, are swiftly laid low. Whole regions such as New England or the North of Britain can, as a result, lose their economic momentum and decline into stagnation and high unemployment. Conversely, less-developed regions which are exposed to competition from the industrially successful and more advanced can remain depressed for decades or even centuries. . . .

For these sectors and regions, which between them comprise the bulk of the world economy, adjustment by unguided market mechanisms is hard and slow. Because of the magnitude of differences among the economies and the pace of economic change, the adjustments required are not marginal but great; and in the real world, as opposed to the classical economic model, such adjustments are slow because the factors of production are not mobile. Capital equipment and skilled manpower are specific to their tasks, and their adaptation to new tasks can be costly, time consuming or impossible. So many industries in the majority of regions face disruption unless the market is guided by controls and adjustment assistance.[15]

In Pinder's view, even if Japan (other countries can now be added) has a long-term comparative advantage in such outputs as ships, steels, and bearings, it makes no sense for the already industrialized countries "to scrap huge investments in capital and skilled manpower and to leave large numbers of workers unemployed for long periods, because of a rate of growth of imports that far exceeds the capacity of these sectors to adjust." Pinder noted that the inherited traditions of an international market system are now on the defensive: "The international system can fight a rearguard action for a time, as it has been doing; but sooner or later, and preferably sooner, the international system will have to be revised to incorporate the durable principles of the new domestic economic management."[16]

The issue is not simply free trade versus managed economy. Most countries, like the United States, are dependent on other nations for certain scarce and strategic resources although the degree of mutual dependence is fluid: substitution, conservation, and abstinence can reduce such needs. However, to secure the necessary imports there must be something to trade, and to trade at prices competitive with

147

those charged by other exporting nations. There is no alternative to developing a sufficient international competitiveness to insure access to vital needs. What is at issue is the extent to which a nation can become more self-reliant, even if at a higher cost, and the desirability of this goal.

And a higher cost is inevitable if a nation pursues this path. Given the emerging shape of world trade, the United States can expect innovation, improved efficiency, and better management to preserve international competitiveness in a number of sectors—but not in enough to provide either full employment or income growth as before. At some point, reality will have to be faced. The home market can be better protected and jobs that under free trade would have been lost to foreign competition can be preserved (though perhaps modified), but output will have to be higher priced; consumer appetites will have to be curbed; and a new style of life with less material indulgence, a different self-perception and value conception, will have to evolve. This is the new mercantilism, toward which the world has in fact been moving rapidly. The 1973 action of the OPEC cartel can be taken as the divide between a world system based on old lines drawn by the West and a new world system whose lines will be determined as much by countries of the South and East. But mercantilism—the political exploitation of a country's economic advantages—is not an argument for either imperialism or protectionism; as Dell reminded us, it is a policy consistent with free trade—when free trade respects the nation's interests.

The new mercantilism does not mean a disintegration of the competitive world market but a much looser association of nations and regions, with the market subordinated to negotiated agreements. Presumably such trade agreements would emerge as the building blocks of a new, more stable, international economic order, less susceptible to disruptions occasioned by the need for ad hoc protectionism. Within such a system, nations and regions could pursue their own domestic policies without threat of retaliation for failure to conform to rules now obsolete:

> The power of nations will in future be determined as much by success in international trade as ever it was, in the old days, by military victories. And just as in the old days military victories were won by alliances, so these days there are mercantilist alliances. . . . The domestic economic policies of major industrialized nations can seriously affect their trading partners, for good or ill; hence

the proliferation of economic summits in which nations try to influence the economic policies of their trading partners who, for similar reasons, try to present their policies as something more than self-regarding.[17]

The emerging international economy is not likely to permit the United States to advance its interests by leaving the multinational corporations to pursue their way as independently as in the past: "The present situation, in which the U.S. national chair remains empty while an important and increasing share of world economic activity is negotiated between multinational enterprises and the governments of host countries, is untenable."[18] The same can be said of the way in which private commercial banks have been allowed to decide, as a matter of private interest, which nations will receive loans and on what terms:

> These commercial transactions to finance balance of payments deficits are having a clear and inevitable foreign policy consequence. Private banks are effectively making United States foreign economic policy without public debate or oversight by elected representatives. Though not part of the contract terms, these private loan agreements require a virtual guarantee of the borrowers' favorable access to markets for their exports so they can earn foreign exchange. In a parody of the 19th-century British colonialism, the United States would become a captive market for products as it became the victim of the foundering debtors.[19]

These international developments are fraught with importance both for the government of nations and for the government of large corporations. The multinational can probably expect its operations to conform more and more to a design drawn between the United States as home base and foreign countries as host. The design would become part of an international mosaic in which the role of U.S. corporation in foreign enterprise would be subject to intergovernmental agreement.

Paul Streeten identified four sequential questions that a developing country must ask itself in formulating a policy toward multinational corporations. A positive answer to each gives rise to the next question:

> (1) Are foreign enterprises wanted at all? Some countries, though their number is declining, may reject outright the idea of foreigners making profits in their country. (2) Is the particular product or

product range wanted? Many products of multinationals are over-specified, overprocessed, overpackaged, oversophisticated, developed for high-income, high-saving markets, produced by capital-intensive techniques and, while catering for the masses in richer countries, can cater for only a small upper crust in poorer countries. (3) Should the product be imported or produced at home? Home production could be for the domestic market or for export. (4) Is direct foreign investment the best way to assemble the package of management, capital, and know-how? The host country has a variety of choices. It can borrow the capital, hire managers, and acquire a license; use domestic inputs for some components of the "package"; or use consultancy services, management contracts, importing houses, or banks. If it is decided that direct foreign investment in the form of multinational subsidiary is the best way of assembling the package, the terms of the negotiation will have to be settled, so that the host country strikes the best bargain, consistent with efficient operation of the multinational.[20]

Obviously, the developing country itself must decide these questions, but in arriving at answers it may be influenced by the attitude of the multinational—and the latter in turn by the interests and inducements of the U.S. government. Streeten suggested that there may well be a conflict "between the basic goods the poor need and the advertised consumer goods of the multinationals." Thus, the new multinationals from the foremost developing countries may better serve Third World needs. The technology they offer may be more appropriate, more labor-intensive, adapted to local supply and social conditions, more responsive to local involvement. They may design "products more adapted to the consumption and production needs of the poor—hoes, simple power tillers, and bicycles, rather than air conditioners, expensive cars, and equipment for luxury apartments."[21]

If this should indeed prove to be the case, the free trader hope of sustaining the West by moving to more and more sophisticated technologies may prove illusory: the present industrialized countries would be left in the position of selling their capital-intensive, sophisticated products to each other, while abandoning one after another the large employing industries adaptable to the low-cost conditions of developing nations. They would rely for strategic raw materials *and* basic goods on those same industrializing nations but would lessen the latter's dependence on them, having exported a technological capability.

Clearly there is a need for a new system of international economic relations in which not the autonomous multinational corporation

—the bugaboo of only a few years back—but the governments of nations, in both the developed and the developing sector, will play the decisive role. The interests of government and corporation are likely to coincide in some respects, but not all. It is even conceivable that the United States might limit certain overseas operations of its major corporations not only in the interests of its own society but also—as a matter of strategic foreign policy—in the interests of the developing countries of the third world, from which it has so far been largely alienated. In any event, the conduct of the large corporation abroad as well as at home may well in the near future be geared to a loosely integrated set of national priorities and reflect a broader sense of social concern, mediated by a changed corporate structure and rewarded by a larger role in the overall design.

Notes

1. Robert Gilpin, *U.S. Power and the Multinational Corporation* (New York: Basic Books, 1975), p. 140.
2. Harry Johnson, quoted in Paul Streeten, "Multinationals Revisited," *Finance and Development*, June 1979, p. 40.
3. *New York Times*, September 18, 1976.
4. Gilpin, *U.S. Power*, p. 138.
5. Ibid., pp. 139–140.
6. Ibid., pp. 141–142.
7. *New York Times*, February 9, 1972.
8. Jack N. Behrman, "Multinational Corporations, Transnational Interests, and National Sovereignty," *Columbia Journal of World Business* 4 (March–April 1969):17.
9. The view of C. Fred Bergsten, Thomas Horst, and Theodore H. Moran, authors of *American Multinational Corporations and American Interests* (Washington, D.C.: Brookings Institution, 1978), cited in *Brookings Bulletin* 15, 2 (1978):9.
10. John Maynard Keynes, "National Self-sufficiency," *Yale Review* 22 (June 1933):757.
11. Ibid., p. 758.
12. Ibid., p. 760.
13. Ibid., p. 762.
14. Edmund Dell, *Political Responsibility and Industry* (London: George Allen & Unwin, 1973). pp. 28, 41.
15. John Pinder, "The New International Economic Disorder and Its Consequences for Italy, *Lo spettatore internazionale* (Rome), no. 2 (1976):106.
16. John Pinder, "Towards a New System of International Management" (mimeo, undated but probably 1976), pp. 5–6.

17. Edmund Dell, "The Politics of Economic Interdependence" (Rita Hinden Memorial Lecture, London, 1977).
18. Bergsten, Horst, and Moran, quoted in *Brookings Bulletin*, p. 9.
19. Jack Zwick and Richard K. Goeltz, "U.S. Banks Are Making Foreign Policy," *New York Times*, March 18, 1979.
20. Streeten, "Multinationals Revisited," pp. 41–42.
21. Ibid., p. 42.

10

Outlook and Perspective

The Conference Board, an organization of major American business firms, sponsors both research into the practices and views of its members with respect to operational problems (budgeting or advertising, affirmative action, organizational principles, work incentives, and productivity) and conferences at which members and invited outsiders discuss social, political and economic influences and effects on corporations.

At a series of eight meetings ending in September 1975, some 360 executives of corporate members gathered to debate the changing relationship between business and society. The president of the Conference Board commented:

> Involved in the discussions . . . were men whose strong conservative bent has only reluctantly been modified by the new social realities. But they were as few in number as were those of such liberal tendencies that they put social goals ahead of the economic objectives of business. The overwhelming majority held the view that the prime goal of business is still to provide people with desired goods and services (and that to continue doing so requires operating profitably). But they believe that this must be done with attention to the social objectives of the public and within the restraints society has imposed. Nor is this a reluctant or even passive attitude for many. They believe businessmen as a group, en-

153

dowed with resources and a capacity to get things done, must take a leadership role in setting and fulfilling social goals.[1]

Asked to provide an independent commentary on the discussions, Leonard Silk, an economist and member of the editorial board of the New York Times, and David Vogel, of the University of California at Berkeley, attended the meetings as objective observers. After ranging over the variety of topics that came under very lively debate, Silk and Vogel offered their conclusion:

> A business community, if it is to assume a position of leadership in society, must somehow generate a vision of purpose that transcends its own role and its own direct and immediate benefits. But such a transcendent vision is extremely difficult for American businessmen to attain, since it appears to conflict with the traditional and deepest American ideology, to which Alexis de Tocqueville, a century and a half ago, gave the name "the philosophy of self-interest." . . .
>
> By clinging to an outmoded ideology, American businessmen and their political representatives are trying to impose solutions that not only fail, but also impede more effective means of dealing with national and international problems. . . . More and more thoughtful business executives, whether because they think it is prudent and necessary or because they think it is right, are trying to form a new philosophy or ideology; or, to put it more plainly, to find a new way of conceiving of their job, of their role, of their mission, of their values, that might lead to a better reconciliation of private objectives and public goals. Their hope is to find a means of safeguarding the relative autonomy of private business while helping to solve urgent public problems which large corporations cannot help but affect one way or the other—for good or evil.[2]

The search for a "means of safeguarding the relative autonomy of private business while helping to solve urgent public problems" has been the focus of this study. The end sought implies a new corporate strategy, a social strategy, that relates the corporation more effectively to society's most fundamental interests. This strategy involves a change in perspective so major as to seem revolutionary, a recognition that while the large corporations have as a principal function the meeting of society's economic needs, their very size and impact can no longer limit them to this function. The argument that profit is needed for survival and that therefore economic motivation must come first is at this time almost meaningless. The

154

survival of corporations is indeed at stake—not only to pursue self-determined operations generating profit but also to pursue social programs enriching society's way of life. Profit is requisite to both functions, but neither maximum profit nor targeted profit nor profit accruing only to a particular segment of the public nor profit freely manipulated by management or realized in traditional ways.

The controversy over the survival of the Chrysler corporation in 1979 and thereafter is indicative of the intellectual marshland through which we are floundering. Some argued that the company could not be allowed to go under—too many jobs were at stake, too many communities were vulnerable. Perhaps shareholders and employees should be asked to take less to qualify the company for government assistance, but the organization should be nursed back to health. Others believed that competitive market principles should be adhered to, and if the company could not succeed on its own it should be allowed to fail. Some plants would be bought up and operated by other concerns, displaced workers would find new jobs after a time, and the company's demise would be simply an incident in the ongoing economic life of the nation. Still others took the position that it would be a mistake to allow an institution that had lasted for decades to go under because at one stage it had failed to read the market rightly; rather, the organization should be held together but its mission modified. Instead of churning out more private cars, which were clearly unneeded given industry capacity and the national concern for resource conservation (making cars last longer, playing down style changes), perhaps the company could turn to designing and producing public transportation vehicles, for example. Obviously, this conversion could not be accomplished overnight, perhaps not within a year or two or five, so that the suggestion was tempting but unpromising. Nevertheless, something of the sort might have been accomplished more expeditiously and less painfully if government and industry had anticipated public needs and priorities. In this event, falling profit would have been an indicator of problems, but a profit sustained simply by doing better what had been done before would solve only a private corporate problem without addressing the larger issue of the role of the automobile industry as a whole vis-à-vis the evolving transportation needs of the nation.

In the Chrysler case there was no structure through which these national policy issues could be examined, no framework including the corporation as an entity, the auto industry, the automobile workers' union, public representatives, or government authorities. The necessary corporate social strategy lacked a structure to accommodate it.

This study has attempted to pull together a number of strands that, integrated, might offer such a structure. I have drawn on the analyses and viewpoints of many people who have given serious attention to various facets of this need. Obviously, other designs are possible. Whatever design may be chosen, the interests and outlooks of the major segments of American society would have to be taken into account. And however the solution is reached, whether by taking small steps over time or by joining together larger building blocks under pressure of circumstance, the result will necessarily—and desirably—emerge in a rather rough and ragged form, rather than as a finished blueprint.

Devising a new structure does not guarantee formulation of the social strategy to be served. Indeed, as we have seen, that strategy has barely begun to take shape. There does, however, seem to be a growing willingness at least to contemplate what once would have been unthinkable—that the autonomous individual, in both consumer and producer roles, can no longer be the fulcrum of our society and that political decisions must provide a framework that goes beyond outlining boundaries for the pursuit of self-interest to promote a social purpose in the very exercise of individual discretion and initiative. This view is doubly radical for it strikes not only at the liberalistic traditions of western society—its Lockean base— but equally at the Marxist thesis, which emphasizes collective decisions lacking private and individual discretion in their realization, locating the same materialistic outlook in the conception of a mechanized society pursuing production goals—a benign machine, simply distributing its products more equitably. In both views, the corporation serves as the efficient instrument of production; only the beneficiaries and controllers differ.

The challenge of a new corporate social strategy lies precisely in recognizing that the production function is not to be carried out as though more efficient distribution were the only goal and as though the criteria for what and how the system produces were to be related primarily to shareholders' advantage. Instead, production would be carried out in a way supportive of national economic priorities and specified social objectives and would in fact be motivated by those objectives as much as by shareholders' benefit. Social objective would not exclude private interest, but neither would private interest take precedence over social objective.

Such a radical shift in view cannot be engineered or even effectively promoted by any corporation acting alone. The competitive market framework precludes that possibility. Therefore, a new social strategy for the corporation would require a structure that embraces economic and social planning and motivates the individual corporation to relate its actions to the larger design. The large corporations may not be compatible with such a realignment—that remains to be seen. What does seem evident is that if such a new social perspective materialized, the large corporations would not be compatible with it as they function today.

The reshaping of social strategy and corporate structure will certainly not come easy. This result may occur only as rehabilitation after debacle. A more hopeful prospect is suggested, however, by the very fact that so many people in positions of authority and responsibility have begun to think seriously about the rigidity and incapacity of the present system of economic, political, and social relations. The more widespread the recognition and concern, the more likely a sense of common need and direction.

If the large corporations are the focus of concern today, from inside as well as outside, and if pressures for change are coming to bear on them because of their strategic importance, other major institutions—for example, government and labor unions—also stand in need of overhaul. So much seems at stake and so much seems to need doing; yet the path ahead is unclear and the wish to hold on to what is familiar is so strong that stalemate may seem a more realistic prospect than change. But that in fact is the least realistic prospect: social problems cannot be laid aside by choice; the pressures build and the old institutional walls will no longer contain them. At some point the forces of change overpower the forces of stasis. What emerges may not be preferable to what is swept away, but that has only a nostalgic relevance. What should concern us now is achieving the best solution of which we are capable, given the forces making for change.

Notes

1. Alexander Trowbridge, foreword to Leonard Silk and David Vogel, *Ethics and Profits* (New York: Simon & Schuster, 1976), pp. 11–12.
2. Ibid., pp. 232–236.

Index

161

Index

About the Author

Neil W. Chamberlain is the Armand G. Erpf Professor (now Emeritus) of the Graduate School of Business, Columbia University. He has also held the chair in management economics in the Department of Economics at Yale University. His professional interests began with industrial relations and labor economics and have subsequently extended to the economics of the firm and corporate planning, national planning, and most recently social values and corporate social responsibility, as reflected in the titles of some of his twenty-two books: *The Union Challenge to Management Control, The Labor Sector, The Firm: Micro-Economic Planning and Action, Private and Public Planning, Enterprise and Environment, The Place of Business in America's Future: A Study in Social Values, The Limits of Corporate Responsibility,* and *Remaking American Values: Challenge to a Business Society.*

He is a past president of the Industrial Relations Research Association and was director of the Program in Economic Development and Administration of the Ford Foundation from 1957 to 1960. He has served on the board of editors of the *American Economic Review*, the editorial council of *Management International*, and the board of trustees of the *Columbia Journal of World Business*.

PROGRAM FOR STUDIES OF
THE MODERN CORPORATION
Graduate School of Business, Columbia University

PUBLICATIONS

*The colophon for this book
as for the other books of the
Program for Studies of the
Modern Corporation was
created by Theodore Roszak*